Augusta J. Evans

Inez

a tale of the Alamo

Augusta J. Evans

Inez
a tale of the Alamo

ISBN/EAN: 9783337072391

Printed in Europe, USA, Canada, Australia, Japan

Cover: Foto ©ninafisch / pixelio.de

More available books at **www.hansebooks.com**

THE WORKS OF
AUGUSTA EVANS WILSON
IN EIGHT VOLUMES

INEZ
A TALE OF THE ALAMO

NEW YORK AND LONDON
THE CO-OPERATIVE PUBLICATION SOCIETY

TO

THE TEXAN PATRIOTS,

WHO TRIUMPHANTLY UNFURLED AND WAVED ALOFT
THE "BANNER OF THE LONE STAR!"

THIS WORK IS RESPECTFULLY DEDICATED

BY THE AUTHOR.

INEZ; A TALE OF THE ALAMO.

CHAPTER I.

*"But O, th' important budget!
Who can say what are its tidings?"*
—*Cowper.*

"THERE is the bell for prayers, Florry; are you ready?" said Mary Irving, hastily entering her cousin's room at the large boarding-school of Madame ———.

"Yes; I rose earlier than usual this morning, have solved two problems, and translated nearly half a page of Télémaque."

"I congratulate you on your increased industry and application, though you were always more studious than myself. I wish, dear Florry, you could imbue me with some of your fondness for metaphysics and mathematics," Mary replied, with a low sigh.

A momentary flush passed over the face of her

companion, and they descended the stairs in silence. The room in which the pupils were accustomed to assemble for devotion was not so spacious as the class-room, yet sufficiently so to look gloomy enough in the gray light of a drizzling morn. The floor was covered with a faded carpet, in which the indistinct vine seemed struggling to reach the wall, but failed by several feet on either side. As if to conceal this deficiency, a wide seat was affixed the entire length of the room, so high

> "That the feet hung dangling down,
> Anxious in vain to find the distant floor."

There were no curtains to the windows, and the rain pattered drearily down the panes.

The teacher who officiated as chaplain was seated before a large desk, on which lay an open Bible. He seemed about twenty-four, his countenance noble rather than handsome, if I may make so delicate a distinction. Intelligence of the first order was stamped upon it, yet the characteristic expression was pride which sat enthroned on his prominent brow; still, hours of care had left their impress, and the face was very grave, though by no means stern. His eye was fixed on the door as the pupils came in, one by one, for prayers, and when Florence and Mary entered, it sunk upon his book. In a few moments he rose, and, standing with one arm folded across his bosom, read in a deep, distinct tone, that beautiful Psalm, "The Lord is my shepherd." He had only reached the fourth verse, when he was interrupted by two girls of twelve or fourteen, who had been conversing from the moment of their entrance. The tones grew louder and louder, and now the words were very audible:

"My father did not send me here to come to prayers, and Madame has no right to make us get up before day to hear him read his Bible!"

Many who coincided with them tittered, others stared in silence, while Florence's lip curled, and Mary looked sorrowingly, pityingly upon them—hers was the expression with which the angel multitudes of Heaven regard their erring brethren here. The chaplain turned toward them, and said, in a grave yet gentle voice, " My little friends, I am afraid you did not kneel beside your bed this morning, and ask God to keep your hearts from sinful thoughts, and enable you to perform all your duties in an humble, gentle spirit. In your present temper, were I to read the entire book instead of one Psalm, I fear you would receive no benefit."

The girls were awed more by the tone than words, and sat silent and abashed. The reading was concluded, and then he offered up a prayer earnest and heart-felt. Instead of leaving the room immediately, the pupils waited as for something, and taking a bundle of letters from the desk, their tutor distributed them as the directions indicated. " My budget is not so large as usual, and I regret it for your sakes, as I fear some are disappointed. Miss Hamilton, here are two for you;" and he handed them to her without looking up.

"Two for Florry, and none for me?" asked Mary, while her voice slightly trembled. He was leaving the room, but turned toward her.

"I am very sorry, Miss Mary, but hope you will find a comforting message in your cousin's."

Gently he spoke, yet his eyes rested on Florence the while, and, with a suppressed sigh, he passed on.

"Come to my room, Mary; it is strange the letters are post-marked the same day." And while she solves the mystery, let us glance at her former history.

CHAPTER II.

"Calm on the bosom of thy God,
 Fair spirit! rest thee now!
Ev'n while with us thy footsteps trod,
 His seal was on thy brow."
—*Hemans.*

FLORENCE HAMILTON had not attained her fourth year when she was left the only solace of her widowed father. Even after the lapse of long years, faint, yet sweet recollections of her last parent stole, in saddened hours, over her spirit, and often, in dreams, a face of angelic beauty hovered around, and smiled upon her.

Unfortunately, Florence proved totally unlike her sainted mother, both in personal appearance and cast of character. Mr. Hamilton was a cold, proud man of the world; one who, having lived from his birth in affluence, regarded with a haughty eye all who, without the advantages of rank or wealth, strove to attain a position equal to his own. Intelligence, nobility of soul, unsullied character, weighed not an atom against the counterpoise of birth and family. He enjoyed in youth advantages rare for the unsettled times in which he lived; he tasted all that France and Italy could offer; and returned *blasé* at twenty-seven to his home in one of the Southern States. Attracted by the brilliant fortune of an orphan heiress, he won and married her, but love, such as her pure, gentle spirit sought, dwelt not in his stern, selfish heart. All of affection he had to bestow was lavished on his only sister, who had married during his absence.

His angel wife drooped in the sterile soil to which she was transplanted, and, when Florence was about four years old, sunk into a quiet grave.

Perhaps when he stood with his infant daughter beside the newly-raised mound, and missed the gentle being who had endeavored so strenuously to make his home happy, and to win for herself a place in his heart, one tear might have moistened the cold, searching eyes that for years had known no such softening tendency. "Perhaps," I say; but to conjecture of thee, oh Man! is fruitless indeed.

As well as such a nature could, he loved his child, and considered himself extremely magnanimous in casting aside all thought of a second marriage, and devoting his leisure moments to the formation of her character and direction of her education.

Florence inherited her father's haughty temperament without his sordid selfishness, and what may seem incompatible with the former, a glowing imagination in connection with fine mental powers. To all but Mr. Hamilton she appeared as cold and impenetrable as himself; but the flashing eye and curling lip with which she listened to a tale of injustice, or viewed a dishonorable act, indicated a nature truly noble. Two master passions ruled her heart —love for her parent, and fondness for books. Idolized by the household, it was not strange that she soon learned to consider herself the most important member of it. Mr. Hamilton found that it was essential for the proper regulation of his establishment that some lady should preside over its various departments, and accordingly invited the maiden sister of his late wife to make his house her home, and take charge of his numerous domestics.

Of his daughter he said nothing. Aunt Lizzy, as she was called, was an amiable, good woman, but not sufficiently intellectual to superintend Florry's education. That little individual looked at first with distrustful eyes on one who, she supposed, might abridge her numerous privileges; but the affectionate manner of the kind-hearted aunt removed all fear, and she soon spoke and moved with the freedom which had characterized her solitude.

One day when Florence was about nine years old,

her father entered the library, where she sat intently reading, and said,

"Florence, come here, I have something to tell you."

"Something to tell me! I hope it is pleasant;" and she laid her hand on his knee, and looked inquiringly in his face.

"You remember the cousin Mary, whose father died not long ago? Well, she has lost her mother too, and is coming to live with us." As he spoke, his voice faltered and his proud curling lip quivered, yet he gave no other evidence of the deepest grief he had known for many years.

"She will be here this evening, and I hope you will try to make her contented." With these words he was leaving the room, but Florence said,

"Father, is she to stay with us always, and will she sleep in my room with me?"

"She will live with us as long as she likes, and if you prefer it, can occupy the same room."

The day wore on and evening found her on the steps looking earnestly down the avenue for the approach of the little stranger.

At length a heavy carriage drove to the door, and Florry leaned forward to catch a glimpse of the inmate's face. A slight form, clad in deep mourning, was placed on the piazza by the coachman.

Mr. Hamilton shook her hand kindly, and after a few words of welcome, said,

"Here is your cousin Florence, Mary. I hope you will love each other, and be happy, good little girls." Mary looked almost fearfully at her proud young cousin, but the sight of her own pale, tearful face touched Florry's heart, and she threw her arms round her neck and kissed her. The embrace was unexpected, and Mary wept bitterly.

"Florence, why don't you take Mary to her room?"

"Would you like to go upstairs, cousin?"

"Oh, yes! if you please, I had much rather." And taking her basket from her hand, Florry led the way.

Mary took off her bonnet and turned to look again at her cousin. Their eyes met; but as if overcome by some sudden recollection, she buried her face in her hands and burst again into tears.

Florence stood for some time in silence, at length she said gently,

"It is almost tea-time and father will be angry if he sees you have been crying."

"Oh! I can't help it, indeed I can't," sobbed the little mourner, "he is so much like my dear, darling mother!" and she stifled a cry of agony.

"Is my father like your mother, cousin Mary?"

"Oh, yes! When he spoke to me just now, I almost thought it was mother."

A tear rolled over Florry's cheek, and she slowly replied, "I wish I knew somebody that looked like my mother." In that hour was forged the chain which bound them through life, and made them one in interests.

Years rolled on, and found Mary happy in her adopted home. If her uncle failed to caress her as her loving heart desired, she did not complain, for she was treated like her cousin, and found in the strong love of Florence an antidote for every care. Mary was about sixteen, and Florence a few months younger, at the time our story opens, and had been placed in New Orleans to acquire French and music, as good masters could not be obtained nearer home. We have seen them there, and hoping the reader will pardon this digression, return to Florry's letter.

CHAPTER III.

"Philosophy can hold an easy triumph over past and future misfortunes; but those which are present, triumph over her."

-Rochefoucault.

A STRIKING difference in personal appearance was presented by the cousins as they stood together. Florence, though somewhat younger, was taller by several inches, and her noble and erect carriage, in connection with the haughty manner in which her head was thrown back, added in effect to her height. Her hair and eyes were brilliant black, the latter particularly thoughtful in their expression. The forehead was not remarkable for height, but was unusually prominent and white, and almost overhung the eyes. The mouth was perfect, the lips delicately chiseled and curving beautifully toward the full dimpled chin. The face, though intellectual, and artistically beautiful, was not prepossessing. The expression was cold and haughty; and for this reason she had received the appellations of " Minerva " and " Juno," such being considered by her fellow-pupils as singularly appropriate.

Mary, on the contrary, was slight and drooping, and her sweet, earnest countenance elicited the love of the beholder even before an intimate acquaintance had brought to view the beautiful traits of her truly amiable character.

And yet these girls, diametrically opposed in disposition, clung to each other with a strength of affection only to be explained by that strongest of all ties, early association.

Florence broke the seal of her letter and Mary walked to the window. It looked out on a narrow street through which drays rattled noisily and occasional passengers picked their way along its muddy crossings.

Mary stood watching the manœuvres of a little girl who was endeavoring to pass dry-shod, when a low groan startled her, and turning quickly she perceived Florence standing in the centre of the room, the letter crumpled in one hand; her face had grown very pale and the large eyes gleamed strangely.

" Oh! Florry, what is the matter? Is your father ill—dead—tell me quick!" and imploringly she clasped her hands.

Florence made a powerful effort and spoke in her usual tone:

"I was foolish to give way to my feelings even for a moment—my father is well." She paused, and then added, as if painfully: "But, oh! he is almost penniless!"

"Penniless!" echoed Mary, as though she could not comprehend her cousin's meaning.

"Yes, Mary, he has been very unfortunate in his speculations, obliged to sell our plantation and negroes, and now, he says, ' a few paltry thousands only remain;' but, oh! that is not the worst—I wish it were; he has sold out everything, broken every tie, and will be here this evening on his way to Texas. He writes that I must be ready to accompany him to-morrow night."

She paused, as if unwilling to add something which must be told, and looked sadly at her cousin.

Mary understood the glance.

"Florry, there is something in the letter relating to myself, which you withhold for fear of giving me pain; the sooner I learn it the better."

"Mary, here is a letter inclosed for you; but first hear what my father says," and hurriedly she read as follows:

. . . "With regard to Mary, it cannot be expected that she should wish to accompany us on our rugged path, and bitterly, bitterly do I regret our separation. Her paternal uncle, now in affluence, has often expressed a desire to have her with him, and since my misfortunes has written me, offering her a home in his family. Every luxury and advantage afforded by wealth can still be hers. Did I not feel that she would be benefited by this separation, nothing could induce me to part with her, but under existing circumstances, I can consent to give her up."

Florence flung the letter from her as she concluded, and approaching her cousin, clasped her arms fondly about her. Mary had covered her face with her hands, and the tears glistened on her slender fingers.

"Oh, Florry! you don't know how pained and hurt I am that uncle should think I could be so ungrateful as to forget, in the moment of adversity, his unvaried kindness for six long years. Oh, it is cruel in him to judge me so harshly," and she sobbed aloud.

"I will not be left, I will go with him, that is if—if—Florry, tell me candidly, do you think he has any other reason for not taking me except my fancied dislike to leaving this place—tell me?"

"No, dear Mary; if he thought you preferred going with us, no power on earth could induce him to leave you."

Mary placed her hand in her cousin's, and murmured:

"Florry, I will go with you; your home shall be my home, and your sorrows my sorrows."

A flash of joy irradiated Florence's pale face as she returned her cousin's warm embrace.

"With you, Mary, to comfort and assist me, I fear nothing; but you have not yet read your uncle's letter; perhaps its contents may influence your decision."

Mary perused it in silence, and then put it in her cousin's hand, while the tears rolled over her cheeks.

"Mary, think well ere you reject this kind offer. Remember how earnestly he entreats that you will come and share his love, his home and his fortune. Many privations will be ours in the land to which we go, and numberless trials assail the poverty-stricken. All these you can avoid by accepting this very affectionate invitation. Think well, Mary, lest in after years you repent your hasty decision."

There came a long pause, and hurriedly Florence paced to and fro. Mary lifted her bowed head, and pushing back her clustering hair, calmly replied, "My heart swells with gratitude toward my noble, generous uncle. Oh, how fervently I can thank him for his proffered home! yet, separated from you, dear Florry, I could not be happy; my heart would ache for you and your warm, trusting love. I fear neither poverty nor hardships. Oh, let me go with you and cheer and assist my dear uncle!"

"You shall go with us, my pure-hearted cousin. When I thought a moment since of parting with you, my future seemed gloomy indeed, but now I know that you will be near I am content."

A short silence ensued, broken by a mournful exclamation from Florence.

"Ah! Mary, it is not for myself that I regret this change of fortune, but for my proud, haughty father, who will suffer so keenly. Oh, my heart aches when I think of him!"

"Florry, we must cheer him by those thousand little attentions which will lead him to forget his pecuniary troubles."

Florence shook her head.

"You do not know my father as I do. He will have no comforts, broods over difficulties in secret, and shrinks from sympathy as from a 'scorching brand.'"

"Still I think we can do much to lighten his cares and I pray God I may not be mistaken," replied Mary.

Florence lifted her head from her palm and gazed vacantly at her cousin, then started from her seat.

"Mary, we must not sit here idly when there is so much to do. Madame —— should know we leave to-morrow, and it will take us all day to prepare for our journey."

"Do let me go and speak to Madame——; it will be less unpleasant to me!"

"No, no; I will go myself: they shall not think I feel it so sensibly, and their condolence to-morrow would irritate me beyond measure. I scorn such petty trials as loss of fortune, and they shall know it."

"Who shall know it, Florry?"

Her cheek flushed, but without a reply she left the room, and descended the steps which led to Madame ——'s parlor. Reaching the door, she drew herself proudly up, then knocked.

"Come in," was the response.

She did so. In the centre of the apartment, with an open book on the table before him sat the teacher who officiated at prayers. He rose and bowed coldly in answer to her salutation.

"Pardon my intrusion, Mr. Stewart. I expected to find Madame here."

"She has gone to spend the morning with an invalid sister, and requested me to take charge of her classes in addition to my own. If I can render you any assistance, Miss Hamilton, I am at your service."

"Thank you, I am in need of no assistance, and merely wished to say to Madame that I should leave New Orleans to-morrow, having heard from my father that he will be here in the evening boat."

"I will inform her of your intended departure as as early as possible."

"You will oblige me by doing so," replied Florence, turning to go.

"Miss Hamilton, may I ask you if your cousin accompanies you?"

"She does," was the laconic answer, and slowly she retraced her steps, and stood at her own door. The cheeks had become colorless, and the delicate lips writhed with pain. She paused a moment, then entered.

"Did you see her, Florry?"

"No, she is absent, but I left word for her."

Her tone was hard, dry, as though she had been striving long for some goal, which, when nearly attained, her failing strength was scarce able to grasp. It was the echo of a fearful struggle that had raged in her proud bosom. The knell it seemed of expiring exertion, of sinking resistance. Mary gazed sadly on her cousin, who stood mechanically smoothing her glossy hair. The haughty features seemed chiseled in marble, so cold, stony was the expression.

"Dear Florry! you look harassed and weary already. Why, why will you overtask your strength, merely to be called a disciple of Zeno? Surely you can not seriously desire so insignificant an honor, if it merits that title?"

"Can you, then, see no glory in crushing long-cherished hopes—nay, when your heart is yearning toward some 'bright particular' path, to turn without one symptom of regret, and calmly tread one just the opposite! Tell me, can you perceive nothing elevating in this Stoical command?"

The cold, vacant look had passed away; her dark eyes gleamed, glittered as with anticipated triumph.

"Florry, I do not understand you exactly; but I do know that command of the heart is impossible, from the source whence you draw. It may seem perfect control now, but it will fail you in the dark hour of your need, if many trials should assail. Oh! my cousin, do not be angry if I say 'you have forsaken the fountain of living water, and hewn out for yourself broken cisterns, which hold no water.' Oh! Florry, before you take another step, return to Him 'who has a balm for every wound.'"

Florence's face softened; an expression of relief began to steal over her countenance; but as Mary ceased speaking, she turned her face, beautiful in its angelic purity, full upon her. A bitter smile curled Florence's lip, and muttering hoarsely, " A few more hours and the struggle will be over," she turned to her bureau, and arranged her clothes for packing.

The day passed in preparation, and twilight found the cousins watching intently at the casement. The great clock in the hall chimed out seven, the last stroke died away, and then the sharp clang of the door bell again broke silence. They started to their feet, heard the street door open and close—then steps along the stairs, nearer and nearer—then came a knock at the door. Mary opened it; the servant handed in a card and withdrew. " Mr. J. A. Hamilton." Florence passed out, Mary remained behind.

" Come, why do you linger ?"

" I thought, Florry, you might wish to see him alone; perhaps he would prefer it."

" Mary, you have identified yourself with us. To my father we must be as one." She extended her hand, and the next moment they stood in the reception room.

The father and uncle was standing with folded arms, looking down into the muddy street below. He advanced to meet them, holding out a hand to each. Florence pressed her lips to the one she held, and exclaimed,

" My dear father, how glad I am to see you!"

"Glad to see me! You did not receive my letters then?"

"Yes I did, but are their contents and pleasure at meeting you incompatible?"

He made no reply, and then Mary said, in a low, tremulous tone,

"Uncle, you have done me a great injury, and you must make me all the reparation in your power. You said, in your letter to Florry, that you did not think I would wish to go with you. Oh, uncle! you do not, can not believe me so ungrateful, so devoid of love as to wish, under any circumstances, to be separated from you. Now ease my heart, and say I may share your new home. I should be very miserable away from you."

An expression of pleasure passed over his face, but again the brow darkened.

"Mary! Florence is my child—my destiny hers, my misfortunes hers; but I have no right to drag you with me in my fall; to deprive you of the many advantages that will be afforded by your uncle's wealth, of the social position you may one day attain."

"Uncle! uncle! am I not your child by adoption? Have you not loved and cared for me during long years? Oh! what do I care for wealth—for what you call a high position in the world? You and Florry are my world." She threw her arms about his neck, and sobbed, "Take me! oh, take me with you!"

"If you so earnestly desire it, you shall indeed go

with us, my Mary." And, for the first time in her life, he imprinted a kiss on her brow.

When he departed, it was with a promise to call for them the next morning, that they might make, with their aunt, some necessary purchases, and remove to a hotel near the river.

Every thing was packed the ensuing day, when Mary suddenly remembered that her books were still in the recitation room, and would have gone for them, but Florence said,

"I will bring up the books, Mary; you are tired and pale with bending so long over that trunk." And accordingly she went.

Mary threw herself on the couch to rest a moment, and fell into a reverie of some length, unheeding the flying minutes, when she recollected that Florence had been absent a long time, and rising, was about to seek her; just then her cousin entered. A change had come over her countenance—peace, quiet, happiness reigned supreme. One hour later, and they had gone from Madame ——'s, never to return again.

CHAPTER IV.

"Time the supreme! Time is eternity,
Pregnant with all eternity can give;
With all that makes archangels smile.
Who murders time, he crushes in the birth
A power ethereal."
— *Young.*

A YEAR had passed away.

Season had followed season in rapid succession, and the last rays of an August sun illumined a scene so beautiful, that I long for the pencil of a Claude Lorraine. It was a far-off town in a far-off state, yet who has gazed on thy loveliness, oh, San Antonio, can ere forget thee! thine was the sweetness of nature; no munificent hand had arranged, with artistic skill, a statue here, a fountain there.

The river wound like an azure girdle round the town; not confined by precipitous banks, but gliding along the surface, as it were, and reflecting, in its deep blue waters, the rustling tule which fringed the margin. An occasional pecan or live-oak flung a majestic shadow athwart its azure bosom, and now and then a clump of willows sighed low in the evening breeze.

Far away to the north stretched a mountain range, blue in the distance; to the south, the luxuriant valley of the stream. The streets were narrow, and wound with a total disregard of the points of the compass. Could a stranger have been placed blindfold in one of them, and then allowed to look about him, the flat roofs and light appearance of most of the houses would have forced him to declare that he had entered a tropical town of the far-east.

Many of the buildings were of musquit pickets, set upright in the ground, lashed together with strips of hide, and thatched with the tule before mentioned. There were scarce three plank-floors in the town; by far the greater number being composed of layers of pebbles, lime, and sand, rolled with a heavy piece of timber till quite compact; daily sprinkling was found necessary, however, to keep down the dust, produced by constant friction.

The wealthy inhabitants built of sun-dried bricks, overcast with a kind of stucco. Yet, unfortunately, the plastering art died with the Montezumas, for the most vivid imagination failed to convert this rough coating into the "silver sheen" which so dazzled Cortes's little band. The reader will exclaim, "I can fancy no beauty from so prosy a description. Thatched roofs and dirt floors, how absurd!"

Although a strict analysis might prove detrimental, I assure you the "*tout ensemble*" was picturesque indeed.

> "Italia! oh Italia! thou who hast
> The fatal gift of beauty,"

art rivaled here! Thy gorgeous skies have floated hither, and hover like a halo round the town. The sun had set; the glowing tints faded fast, till of the brilliant spectacle naught remained save the soft, roseate hue which melted insensibly into the deep azure of the zenith. Quiet seemed settling o'er mountain and river, when, with a solemn sweetness, the vesper bells chimed out on the evening air. Even as the Moslem kneels at sunset toward the " Holy City," so punctiliously does the devout papist bend for vesper prayers. Will you traverse with me the crooked streets, and stand beneath the belfry whence issued the holy tones?

This ancient edifice was constructed in 1692. It fronted the Plaza, and was a long, narrow building, flanked, as it were, by wings lower than the main apartment, and surmounted by a dome, in which were five or six bells. This dome or belfry was supported by pillars, and in the intervening openings were placed the bells. The roof was flat, and the dark green and gray moss clung along the sides. The interior presented a singular combination of art and rudeness; the seats were of unpainted pine, and the cement floor between was worn irregularly by the knees of devout attendants. The railing of the altar was of carved mahogany, rich and beautiful. Over this division of the long room hung a silken curtain, concealing three niches, which contained an image of the " Virgin," the " Child," and in the centre one, a tall gilt cross. Heavy silver candlesticks were placed in front of each niche, and a dozen candles were now burning dimly. A variety of relics, too numerous to mention, were scattered on the altar, and in addition, several silver goblets, and a massive bowl for holding "holy water." A few tin sconces, placed against the wall, were the only provision for lighting that dark, gloomy church, and dreary enough it looked in the twilight hour. About a dozen devotees were present, all kneeling on the damp, hard floor. The silk curtain which concealed the altar was drawn aside, with due solemnity, by two boys habited in red flannel petticoats, over which hung a loose white slip. The officiating priest was seen kneeling before the altar, with his lips pressed to the foot of the cross. He retained his position for several moments, then rising, conducted the ceremonies in a calm, imposing manner. When these were concluded, and all had departed, save the two boys, who still knelt before the Virgin, he beckoned them to him, and speaking a few words in Spanish, ended by pointing to the door and uttering emphatically, " go !" Crossing themselves as they passed the images, they disappeared through a side door, and the priest was left alone.

CHAPTER V.

> * * * "He was a man
> Who stole the livery of the court of heaven
> To serve the devil in; in Virtue's guise,
> Devoured the widow's house and orphan's bread;
> In holy phrase, transacted villanies
> That common sinners durst not meddle with."
> —*Pollok.*

In years, he could not have exceeded twenty-five, yet the countenance was that of one well versed in intrigue. The cast was Italian—the crisp black hair, swarthy complexion, and never-to-be-mistaken eyes. A large amount of Jesuit determination was expressed in his iris, blended with cunning, malignity, and fierceness. The features were prominent, particularly the nose; the lips finely cut, but thin; the teeth beautiful and regular. In stature he was low, and habited in the dress of his order, a long black coat or gown, buttoned to the throat, and reaching nearly to the feet.

Glancing at his watch as the sound of the last step died away, he paced round and round the altar, neglecting now the many genuflections, bows, and crossings with which he had honored the images in the presence of his flock. His brows were knit, as if in deep thought, and doubtless he revolved the result of some deep laid plan, when the door was hurriedly opened, and a man, bowing low before the images, approached him. The dress of the stranger declared him a ranchero: he wore no jacket, but his pantaloons were of buckskin, and his broad sombrero was tucked beneath his arm.

"Benedicite, Juan!"

"Bueño noche, Padre.

"What tidings do you bring me?" said Father Mazzolin.

The Mexican handed him a letter, and then, as if much fatigued, leaned heavily against the wall, and wiped his brow with a large blue cotton handkerchief. As the priest turned away and perused his letter, a smile of triumphant joy irradiated his face, and a momentary flush tinged his dark cheek. Again he read it, then thrusting it into his bosom, addressed the bearer:

"May the blessing of the church rest upon you, who have so faithfully served your Padre;" and he extended his hand. Warmly it was grasped by Juan, with a look of grateful surprise.

"Este bueño?" inquired Juan.

"Si mui bueño. Juan, do you read American writing?"

"Chiquito," was answered, with a slight shrug.

"What is the news in the el grand Ciudad?"

"They have a strong ox to pull the ropes, now Santa Anna is at the head. 'Bravura!'" and the ranchero tossed his hat, regardless of the place.

It was, however, no part of Mazzolin's policy to allow him for one moment to forget the reverence due the marble images that looked so calmly down from their niches, and with a stern glance he pointed to them, crossing himself as he did so. Juan went down on his knees, and with an " Ave Maria," and a Mexican dollar (which he laid on the altar), quieted his conscience.

" Señor Austin is in the Calaboose," he said, after a pause.

Mazzolin started, and looked keenly at him, as if striving to read his inmost thoughts.

" You must be mistaken, Juan; there is no mention of it in my letter!" he said, in a tone of one fearing to believe good news.

" Not at all, Padre. We started together—there were fifteen of us—and after we had come a long way, so far as Saltillo, some of Santa Anna's cavaleros overtook us, and carried Señor Americano back with them, and said they had orders to do it, for he was no friend to our nation. I know, for I heard for myself."

" Do you know the particular reason of his arrest ?"

Juan shook his head, and replied, " That the officers did not say."

" Did you mention to any one your having a letter for me ?"

" No, Padre; I tell no man what does not concern him."

" A wise plan, Juan, I would advise you always to follow; and be very careful that you say nothing to any one about my letter: I particularly desire it."

" Intiendo," said Juan, turning toward the door. " I go to my ranche to-morrow, but come back before many sunsets, and if you want me again, Padre, you know where to find me."

"The blessing of the 'Holy Virgin' rest upon you, my son, and reward you for your services in behalf of the church."

"Adios!" And they parted.

Father Mazzolin drew forth the letter, and read it attentively for the third time, then held it over one of the twelve candles, and deliberately burnt it, muttering the while, "Ashes tell no tales."

Extinguishing the candles and locking the door of the church, he said to himself:

"All is as I foresaw; a breach is made which can only be closed by the bodies of hundreds of these cursed heretics; and Santa Anna is blood-thirsty enough to drain the last drop. Alphonso Mazzolin, canst thou not carve thy fortune in the coming storm? Yea, and I will. I am no unworthy follower of Loyola, of Xavier, and of Bobadillo. Patience! a Cardinal's cap shall crown my labors;" and with a chuckling laugh he entered the narrow street which led to his dwelling.

"There is but one obstacle here," he continued; "that Protestant girl's work is hard to undo;" and his step became quicker. "But for her, I should have been confessor to the whole family, and will be yet, despite her warning efforts, though I had rather deal with any three men. She is as untiring as myself." He reached his door, and entered.

CHAPTER VI.

"And ruder words will soon rush in
To spread the breach that words begin,
And eyes forget the gentle ray
They wore in courtship's smiling day;
And voices lose the tone that shed
A tenderness round all they said."

—*Moore.*

INEZ DE GARCIA was an only child, and in San Antonio considered quite an heiress. Her wealth consisted in broad lands, large flocks, and numerous herds, and these valuable possessions, combined with her beautiful face, rendered her the object of considerable attention. Inez was endowed with quick perceptions, and a most indomitable will, which she never surrendered, except to accomplish some latent design; and none who looked into her beautiful eyes could suppose that beauty predominated over intellect. She was subtile, and consciousness of her powers was seen in the haughty glance and contemptuous smile. Her hand had been promised from infancy to her orphan cousin, Mañuel Nevarro, whose possessions were nearly as extensive as her own. Inez looked with indifference on her handsome cousin, but never objected, till within a few weeks of her seventeenth birthday (the period appointed for her marriage), when she urged her father to break the engagement. This he positively refused to do, but promising, at Father Mazzolin's suggestion, that she should have a few more months of freedom, she apparently acquiesced. Among the peculiar customs of Mexicans was a singular method of celebrating St. ——'s day. Instead of repairing to their church and engaging in some rational service, they mounted their half wild ponies, and rode furiously up and down the streets till their jaded steeds refused to stir another step, when they were graciously allowed to finish the day on the common. The celebration of the festival was not confined to the masculine portion of the community; silver-haired Señoras mingled in the cavalcade, and many a bright-eyed Señorita looked forward to St. ——'s day with feelings nearly akin to those with which a New York belle regards the most fashionable ball of the season.

On the evening preceding the day of that canonized lady, Mañuel entered the room where Inez sat, her needlework on the floor at some distance, as though flung impatiently from her, her head resting on one hand, while the other held a gentleman's glove. Light as was his step, she detected it, and thrusting the glove into her bosom, turned her fine face full upon him.

"What in the name of wonder brings you here this time of day, Mañuel? I thought every one but myself was taking a siesta this warm evening."

"I have been trying a new horse, Inez, and came to know at what hour you would ride to-morrow."

He stood fanning himself with his broad sombrero as he spoke.

"Excuse me, Señor, I do not intend to ride at all."

"You never refused before, Inez: what is the meaning of this?" and his Spanish brow darkened ominously.

"That I do not feel inclined to do so, is sufficient reason."

"And why don't you choose to ride, pray? You have done it all your life."

"I'll be cross-questioned by no one!" replied Inez, springing to her feet, with flashing eyes, and passionately clinching her small, jeweled hand.

Mañuel was of a fiery temperament, and one of the many who never pause to weigh the effect of their words or actions. Seizing her arm in no gentle manner, he angrily exclaimed:

"A few more weeks and I'll see whether you indulge every whim, and play the queen so royally!"

Inez disengaged her arm, every feature quivering with scorn.

"To whom do you speak, Señor Nevarro? You have certainly mistaken me for one of the miserable peons over whom you claim jurisdiction. Allow me to undeceive you. I am Inez de Garcia, to whom you shall never dictate, for I solemnly declare, that from this day the link which has bound us from childhood is at an end. Mine be the hand to sever it. From this hour we meet only as cousins! Go find a more congenial bride!"

"Hold, Inez! are you mad?'

"No, Mañuel, but candid; for eight years I have known that I was destined to be your wife, but I never loved you, Mañuel. I do not, and never can, otherwise than as a cousin."

In a tone of ill-suppressed rage, Nevarro retorted:

"My uncle's authority shall compel you to fulfill the engagement! You shall not thus escape me!"

"As you please, Señor. Yet let me tell you, compulsion will not answer. The combined efforts of San Antonio will not avail—they may crush, but can not conquer me." She bowed low, and left the room.

Every feature inflamed with wrath, Nevarro snatched his hat, and hurried down the street. He had not proceeded far, when a hand was laid upon his arm, and turning, with somewhat pugnacious intentions, he encountered Father Mazzolin's piercing black eyes.

"Bueño tarde, Padre."

The black eyes rested on Nevarro with an expression which seemed to demand an explanation of his choler. Mañuel moved uneasily; the hot blood glowed in his swarthy cheek, and swelled like cords on the darkened brow.

"Did you wish to speak with me, Padre?"

"Even so, my son. Thou art troubled, come unto one who can give thee comfort."

They were standing before the door of the harkell occupied by the priest; he opened it, and drew Mañuel in.

An hour later they emerged from the house. All trace of anger was removed from Nevarro's brow, and Father Mazzolin's countenance wore the impenetrable cast he ever assumed in public. It was his business expression, the mask behind which he secretly drew the strings, and lured his dupes into believing him a disinterested and self-denying pastor. whose only aim in life was to promote the welfare and happiness of his flock.

When Don Garcia sat that night, *à la Turk*, on a buffalo-robe before his door, puffing his cigarrita, and keeping time to the violin, which sent forth its merry tones at a neighboring fandango, Inez drew near, and related the result of her interview with Mañuel, concluding by declaring her intention to abide by her decision, and consult her own wishes in the selection of a husband.

His astonishment was great. First he tried reasoning, but she refuted every argument advanced with the adroitness of an Abelard: the small stock of patience with which "Dame Nature" had endowed the Don gave way, and at last, stamping with rage, he swore she should comply, or end her life in a gloomy cell of San Jose.

Inez laughed contemptuously. She felt the whirlwind she had raised gathering about her, yet sought not to allay it; she knew it was the precursor of a fierce struggle, yet quailed not. Like the heroine of S ragossa, or the martyr of Rouen, she knew not fear; and her restless nature rather joyed in the strife.

A low growl from the dog who shared the robe, announced an intruder, and the next moment the Padre joined them. He was joyfully hailed by De Garcia as an ally; but a dark look of hatred gleamed from Inez's eyes, as they rested on his form: it vanished instantly, and she welcomed him with a smile. She was cognizant of his interview with Nevarro, for her window overlooked the street in which it took place. She knew, too, his powers of intrigue; that they were enlisted against her; and a glance sufficed to show the path to be pursued. Long ago her penetrating eye had probed the mask of dissimulation which concealed, like the "silver vail" of Mokanna, a great deformity; how much greater because, alas! a moral one.

Father Mazzolin inquired, with apparent interest, the cause of contention. The Don gave a detailed account, and wound up by applying to him for support, in favor of Nevarro. The look of sorrowful astonishment with which he listened, compelled Inez to fix her large Spanish eyes on the ground, lest he should perceive the smile which lurked in their corners, and half played round her lip.

He rebuked her gently, and spoke briefly of the evils which would result, if she persisted in her willful and ungrateful course. Inez listened with a meekness which surprised both parent and Padre; and when the latter rose to go, approached, and, in a low tone, requested him to meet her, that day week, in the confessional.

Woman's heart is every where the same, and in

the solitude of her own apartment, Inez's softer feelings found full vent. She sat with her face in her hands, one long deep sigh, which struggled up, telling of the secret pain that was withering her joys and clouding her future. Suddenly she started up, and passionately exclaimed,

"It is hard that *his* love should be wasted on one whose heart is as cold and stony as this wall;" and she struck it impatiently. Then drawing forth the glove, which on Mañuel's entrance had been so hastily secreted, she pressed it repeatedly to her lips, returned it to its hiding-place and sought her couch.

CHAPTER VII.

"What cause have we to build on length of life:
Temptations seize when fear is laid asleep;
And ill-foreboded is our strongest guard."
— *Young*.

St. ——'s dawn was welcomed by joyous peals from the church-bells, and the occasional firing of a few muskets, by way of accompaniment. The sun rose with a brilliance which would have awakened deep tones in Memnon's statue, and gilded mountain and valley. Beautiful beyond description the city looked in his golden light, and

"All nature seemed rejoicing."

Half hid by a majestic live-oak which shaded the front, and within a few yards of the river, stood a small white house. It was built of adobes, and contained only three rooms. Instead of reaching these by a broad flight, one step from the threshold placed you on the ground. The floor was covered, and, as usual, of cement. In one corner of the front apartment stood a side-board with glass of various kinds, and a few handsome pieces of plate. Its *vis-à-vis* was a range of shelves, filled with books; and on the plain deal mantel-piece stood a pair of neat China vases, decked with brilliant prairie flowers. Before the open window was placed the table, arranged for the morning meal. How pure the cloth looked, how clear the glass; and then the bouquet of fragrant roses which adorned the centre, how homelike, fresh, and beautiful it seemed! An air of comfort, American, southern comfort—pervaded the whole. The breakfast was brought in by a middle-aged negress, whose tidy appearance, and honest, happy, smiling face presented the best refutation of the gross slanders of our northern brethren. I would that her daguerreotype, as she stood arranging the dishes, could be contrasted with those of the miserable, half-starved seamstresses of Boston and New York, who toil from dawn till dark, with aching head and throbbing heart, over some weary article, for which they receive the mighty recompense of a shilling.

When she had arranged every dish with great exactness, a small bell was rung; and, waiter in hand, she stood ready to attend the family.

A bright, young face appeared at the open window.

"I hope, Aunt Fanny, you have a nice breakfast. You have no idea what an appetite my walk has given me."

"Now, Miss Mary, ain't my cooking always nice?"

"Indeed, it is. Your coffee would not disgrace a pacha's table; and your rolls are

'The whitest, the lightest, that ever were seen.'"

She disappeared from the window, and entered the room just as Mr. Hamilton came in, followed by Florence.

"My dear uncle, have you forgotten the old adage of 'early to bed, add early to rise?'"

"I am not sure that I ever learned it, Mary;" he drily replied, seating himself at the table.

"One would suppose you had taken a draught from the 'Elixir of Life;'" said Florence, glancing affectionately at her beaming face.

"I have discovered the fountain of perpetual youth, so vainly sought in South America!"

"Indeed! Is it located in this vicinity?"

"Yes; and if you will rise to-morrow with Aurora, when 'she sprinkles with rosy light the dewy lawn,' I will promise to conduct you to it."

"Thank you; but Mary, what induced you to ramble so early?"

"I have been nearly two miles for some roots Mrs. Carlton expressed a wish for. See, Florry, how I have dyed my hands pulling them up!"

"Were you alone, Mary?" asked Mr. Hamilton.

"I was, most of the time. As I came back, Dr. Bryant overtook me. He spent the night at San Jose mission, with a sick Mexican, and was returning. But where is Aunt Lizzy?" continued Mary, with an inquiring glance round the room.

"She went to mass this morning," replied her cousin.

"Oh, yes! It is St. ——'s day. I heard the bells at daybreak."

"It is a savage, heathenish custom they have adopted here, of tearing up and down the streets from morning till night. I wish, by Jove! they would ride over their canting Padre! I think he would find some other mode of celebrating the festival!"

"He would lay claim to saintship on the strength of it," replied Mary.

"You had better keep out of the street to-day, girls," rejoined Mr. Hamilton, pushing his cup away, and rising from the table.

At this moment Aunt Lizzy entered; and after the morning salutation, turned toward the door.

"You are later than usual this morning, aunt. Do sit down and eat your breakfast, or it will be so cold you can not touch it," said Mary.

"No really devout Catholic tastes food on this holy day," she answered, motioning it from her.

"It must be quite a penance to abstain, after your long walk," said Mr. Hamilton with a smile.

"Father Mazzolin said, this morning, that all who kept this holy day would add a bright jewel to their crown, and obtain the eternal intercession of the blessed saint;" and she left the room.

"That falsehood adds another stone to the many that will sink him in the lake of perdition, if there be one!" muttered Mr. Hamilton, as he departed for the counting-room. The last few sentences had fallen unheeded on Florence's ear, for she sat looking out the window, her thoughts evidently far away. But every trace of merriment vanished from Mary's face, and instead of her bright smile, a look of painful anxiety settled there. A long silence ensued; Mary stood by the table, wiping the cups as Aunt Fanny rinsed them, and occasionally glancing at her cousin. At length she said,

"Florry, will you walk over to Mrs. Carlton's with me? I promised to go, and the walk will do you good, for indeed your cheeks are paler than I like to see them."

"Certainly, Mary, but do you remember what father said about our remaining at home to-day?"

"There is no danger, Florry, if we only look about us; and I really must go."

"Well then, let us start at once."

In a few moments they set out, equipped in large straw hats, and equally large gloves; in addition, Mary carried in her hand a basket filled with herbs and flowers.

"If we walk briskly, we shall get there before any of the riders set forth. Ah! I am mistaken, there they come. Florry, don't go so near the street: that horseman in blue looks as though he were riding on ice—see how his horse slides about!"

A party of twenty or thirty thundered past, and the girls quickened their pace. A few minutes' walk brought them to Mrs. Carlton's door, which closed after them.

That lady was reading, as they entered, but threw aside her book, and advanced joyously to greet them. She kissed Mary affectionately, and cordially shook Florence's hand.

" I am glad you came, Mary. I feared you would not, and really I want you very much."

" What can I do, Mrs. Carlton?"

" You can take off your hat and gloves, and prepare yourselves to spend the day with me."

They laughingly complied, protesting, however, that they could only remain a short time.

" Mary, my poor blind proselyte died yesterday, and bequeathed her orphan child to me: I feel almost obliged to accept the charge, for her fear lest it should fall into the Padre's hands was painful to behold, and I promised to protect it, if possible. The poor little fellow is nearly destitute of clothes; I have cut some for him, and knew you would assist me in making them."

" With pleasure, dear Mrs. Carlton, and so will Florry; fill my basket with work, and we will soon have him a suit. Oh! how glad I am that he has such kind friends as yourself and husband."

" The Padre came last night to demand the child, but we refused to give him up: he said he intended clothing and educating the boy free of charge; yet I knew better, for he refused to baptize Madame Berara's orphan-niece without the customary fee, though he well knew she could ill afford it, and was compelled to sell her last cow to make up the requisite sum. I feel assured he will do all in his power to entice Erasmo from me; but hope by constant watchfulness to counteract his influence. Oh! Mary, how much we need a Protestant minister here: one who could effectually stem the tide of superstition and degradation that now flows unimpeded through this community. Oh! my dear friend, let us take courage, and go boldly forth in the cause of truth, and strive to awaken all from the lethargy into which they have fallen—a lethargy for which their priests are alone responsible, for they administered the deadly drug."

"I feel as deeply as yourself, dear Mrs. Carlton, the evil tendency and deplorable consequences of the institutions by which we are surrounded, and the little that I can do will be gladly, oh how gladly! contributed to the work of reformation you have so nobly begun."

"You forget, Mary, in your proselyting enthusiasm, that Aunt Lizzy belongs to the despised sect; surely you can not intend by attacks on her religion to render her home unpleasant?" said Florence.

Mary's eyes filled with tears, as she glanced reproachfully at her cousin, and replied,

"Nothing is further from my wishes, Florry, than to make her home other than happy. Aunt Lizzy has every opportunity of informing herself on this important question. Yet she prefers the easier method, of committing her conscience to the care of the priest; she has chosen her path in life, and determinately closes her eyes to every other. The state of the Mexicans around us is by no means analogous. They were allowed no choice. Bred from infancy in the Romish faith, they are totally unacquainted with the tenets of other creeds. Implicit obedience to the Padre is their primary law, the grand ruling principle of life, instilled from their birth. To lay before them the truths of our own 'pure and undefiled religion,' is both a privilege and duty."

"You spoke just now, Miss Florence, of the 'despised sect;' allow me, in all modesty, to say, that to the true and earnest Christian there is no such class. Believe me, when I say, that though deeply commiserating their unhappy condition, and resolved to do all in my power to alleviate it, still I would as cheerfully assist the conscientious Papist, and tender him the hospitalities of my home, as one of my own belief."

"You have expressed my feelings exactly, Mrs. Carlton, and there are times when I wish myself a missionary, that I might carry light to this benighted race," exclaimed Mary, enthuiastically.

"We are very apt, my dear child, to consider ourselves equal to emergencies, and capable of great actions, when a strict examination would declare that the minor deeds and petty trials which test the temper and the strength too often destroy our equanimity, and show our inability to cope with difficulties. Woman's warfare is with little things, yet we are assured by the greatest of all female writers, that ' trifles make the sum of human things;' therefore, let us strive more and more earnestly to obtain perfect control of ourselves; then shall we be enabled to assist others."

" I often think," replied Mary, thoughtfully, " that we make great sacrifices with comparative ease, because we feel our own insufficiency, and rely more on God for assistance; while in lesser troubles we are so confident of success, that we neglect to ask his blessing, and consequently fail in our unaided attempts."

" You are right, Mary, and it should teach us to distrust our powers, and lead us to lean upon ' Him, who is a very precious help in time of need.' "

A long silence ensued, broken at length by the entrance of Mrs. Carlton's two children, who carried a large basket between them. Hastily they set it down, seeing Mary, and sprung to her side: the little girl clung around her neck, and kissed her repeatedly.

" Maria, you are too boisterous, my little girl; Miss Mary will have no cause to doubt your affection. Elliot, why do you not speak to Miss Florence, my son ?"

Blushing at his oversight, the boy obeyed, and, joined by his sister, stood at his mother's side. Maria whispered something in his ear; but he only shook his head and replied,

"Not now, sister, let us wait."

She hesitated a moment, then laid her little hand on Mrs. Carlton's shoulder:

"Mother, I know you said it was rude to whisper in company, but I want to tell you something very much."

Mrs. Carlton smiled.

"I am sure the young ladies will excuse you, my daughter, if it is important." She bent her head, and a prolonged whispering followed. A flush rose to the mother's cheek and a tear to her eyes, as she clasped her to her heart, and said:

"I wish you, my children, to speak out, and tell all you know of this affair."

Elliot was spokesman.

"We went into the garden as you desired us, mother, and Erasmo and I picked the peas, while sister held the basket; presently we heard a noise in the brush fence like something coming through, and sister got frightened (here he laughed), and wanted to run to the house, but we told her it was only a sheep or dog outside; but it turned out to be the Padre, and he came and helped us to pick. Mother, he told us such pretty stories; I can't think of the names; they must have been Dutch, they were so long and hard. But I remember one of the tales; he said there was once a good man who lived in Asia, and one day he lost his crucifix; he looked every where for it, but could not find it; and a long time afterward, he happened to be walking by the sea-shore and looked out on the water, and oh, what do you think? He saw his crucifix moving on the water, and a great crab paddled out to land and laid his crucifix down before him, and then paddled right back into the sea again. Now wasn't that funny. I can't think of the good man's name, Saint—Somebody—Saint—Saint——"

"Brother, I reckon it was Saint Crab!"

"No, no! It was the crab that found the crucifix, and I think he was smarter than the Saint."

"Now, Florry, should I repeat this legend to Aunt Lizzy, it would be impossible to convince her that it proceeded from the Padre's lips. Yet even prelates of Rome scruple not to narrate as miracles tales equally absurd, where their auditory is sufficiently ignorant to credit them. Pardon my interruption, Elliot, and finish your story," continued Mary.

"Mother, the Padre talked to Erasmo in Spanish. I could not understand all he said, but it was about coming to live with him, and going to Mexico, to see the sights there. When he came to the rows you left for seed, I told him we must come to the house, and asked him to come in; but he would not, and offered us all some money, and said we must not tell a soul we had seen him, for he happened to see us through the fence, and just came in to speak to us, and you and father might think he ought not to come into our garden. But oh, mother, would you believe it! he told Erasmo, as he went off, that he **must ask you** to let him go to bathe to-morrow; and instead of going to the river, he must come to the church: he wanted to give him something. He told him in Spanish, but I understood what he said. Now wasn't that teaching him to tell a lie? and he a Padre too! Mother, don't you think he ought to be ashamed?"

"Elliot, if you would gladden the hearts of your father and mother, be ever truthful. Remember the story of 'Pedro and Francisco' you read not long ago, and put dishonesty and dissimulation far from you: 'honesty is the best policy,' and if you adhere to it through life, it will prove of 'far more worth than gold.' Be sure you keep nothing from me, particularly what the Padre may say."

"Shall we take the peas out under the hackberry and shell them?" said Maria.

"Yes, my dear, but first tell me where Erasmo is."

"Sitting on the steps, mother. I know he will help us to shell them, for he said it was mere fun picking peas."

"Say nothing to him of the Padre or his conversation, but interest him about other things."

They left the room swinging the basket between them. Mrs. Carlton's eyes filled as she looked after her children. "A mother's care can do a great deal, yet how little did I imagine that temptation would assail them at such a time, and in such a garb."

"Oh, guard them carefully; for, surrounded by these influences, it will be difficult to prevent contamination," said Mary, earnestly.

Just then a loud shout from the street attracted their attention, and hastening to the door, they perceived a crowd gathered on the Plaza. In the centre was a body of Mexican cavalry, headed by their commanding officer, who, hat in hand, was haranguing them. The ladies looked at each other in dismay.

" To what does this tend?" asked Mary, anxiously.

" My husband told me several days since that Austin was imprisoned in Mexico, and said he feared difficulties would ensue, but knew not the cause of his confinement."

" There is Dr. Bryant coming towards us; I dare say he can tell us the meaning of this commotion."

That gentleman, bowing low in the saddle, reined his steed as near the step as possible.

" How do you do, Miss Hamilton, and you, my dear sister? I had the pleasure of meeting Miss Mary in her morning rambles; she is a most remarkable young lady. Assures me she actually loves early rising." His dark eyes were fixed laughingly upon her.

" Do stop your nonsense, Frank, and tell us the cause of that crowd," said Mrs. Carlton laying her hand on his arm.

" My dear sister, that tall, cadaverous-looking cavalier is the brother-in-law of Santa Anna, and no less a personage than General Cos, sent hither to fortify this and every other susceptible place."

" Against whom or what?"

" It is a long story, ladies. You know that Coahuila

has pursued an oppressive policy toward us for some time, and refused to hear reason; Austin remonstrated again and again, and at last went to Mexico, hoping that the authorities would allow us (here he bit his lip, and his cheek flushed)—it galls my spirit to utter the word—allow us to form a separate State. The Congress there took no notice of his petition, for, in truth, they were too much engaged just then about their own affairs to heed him, and he wrote to several persons in Austin, advising them at all hazards to proceed. Some cowardly wretch, or spy in disguise, secretly despatched one of his letters to the ministers; consequently, as Austin was returning, they made him prisoner, and carried him back to Mexico. Santa Anna is at the head of affairs. He has subverted the too liberal constitution of 1824, but is opposed by a few brave hearts, who scorn the servitude in store for them. Santa Anna knows full well that we will not submit to his crushing yoke, and therefore sends General Cos to fortify the Alamo. This is the only definite information I have been able to glean from several sources."

"Do you think there is probability of a war?"

"It will most inevitably ensue, for total submission will be exacted by Santa Anna, and the Texans are not a people to comply with any such conditions."

"You think General Cos is here to fortify the Alamo?"

"Yes; the work commences to-morrow, I hear, and the fort will be garrisoned by Spanish troops."

"How many has he with him?" inquired his sister.

"Only fifty or sixty; this is merely the advanced guard, and the main body will probably arrive in a few days."

"I suppose they are joyously welcomed by the Mexicans here, who have ever regarded with jealous eyes Protestant settlers."

"Oh, yes, that shout testified the hearty welcome they received."

At this moment Mr. Hamilton joined the group.

"Have you heard the news?" he inquired.

"Yes, and sad enough it is," said Mary with a sigh.

"It will be a bloody conflict."

"I am afraid so," replied Dr. Bryant.

"Come, girls, I am going home, will you go now?"

Mary took her basket, which Mrs. Carlton had filled with work, and they descended the steps.

"I declare, Miss Irving, I have a great desire to know what that basket contains; it is as inseparably your companion as was the tub of Diogenes. I often see it round a corner before you are visible, and at the glimpse of it, invariably sit more erect in saddle and assume my most amiable expression."

He raised himself and peeped inquiringly over the edge; Mary swung it playfully behind her.

"I never gratify idle curiosity, Dr. Bryant."

"Indeed, how very remarkable; but I assure you I know full well the use to which those same herbs you had this morning are to be applied; you are amalgamating nauseous drugs and certain pills to be administered to my patients. I am grieved to think you would alienate what few friends I have here, by raising yourself up as a competitor. Pray, where did you receive your diploma? and are you Thomsonian, Allopathic, Homeopathic, or Hydropathic?"

Mary looked at Mrs. Carlton; both smiled.

"Ah! I see Ellen is associated with you. Do admit me to partnership; I should be a most valuable acquisition, take my word for it. A more humble-minded, good-hearted, deeply-read, and experienced disciple of Esculapius never felt pulse or administered a potion."

They laughed outright.

"Mary, shall we tell Frank what we intend those herbs for?"

"By no means; he does not deserve to know."

"Ah! I see Terence was right after all in his opinion of woman's nature—'When you request, they refuse; when you forbid, they are sure to do it.'"

"Come, girls, come! I have business at home;" said Mr. Hamilton, and they set out homeward. They had not proceeded far when Mary exclaimed, pointing behind her:

"Oh, uncle, that woman will be killed! Can nobody help her?"

"She will certainly be thrown from her horse!"

A party of five or six Mexicans were riding with their usual rapidity toward them. An elderly woman in the rear had evidently lost control of her fiery horse which was plunging violently. The other members of the company seemed unable to render any assistance, as their own could scarcely be restrained. The unfortunate Señora was almost paralyzed with fright; for instead of checking him by the reins, they had fallen over his head, become entangled in his feet, and now grasping the mane, she was shrieking fearfully.

"Oh, can't we do something for her!" cried Mary, clasping her hands.

"I do not see how we can assist her," said Mr. Hamilton.

"At least let us try;" and they hastened to the spot where the infuriated animal was struggling.

"Stand back, girls! you can do nothing."

He made several ineffectual attempts to catch the bridle as the fore-feet rose in the air, and at last succeeded in getting one end. He bade the woman let go the mane and slide off. She did so, but some portion of her dress was caught in the saddle, and she hung suspended. The horse, feeling the movement, again plunged, despite Mr. Hamilton's efforts to hold him down. The scene was distressing indeed, as she was raised and then flung down again.

Mary saw the danger, and rushing round the enraged horse, fearlessly pushed off the piece which was attached to the pommel of the saddle, and freed the unfortunate matron. The horse, feeling relieved of his burden, gave a desperate bound and rushed off down the street.

Florence shrieked and sprung to her father's side.

Mary was bending over the moaning woman, but turned suddenly and saw her uncle stretched at Florence's feet. He was insensible, and a stream of blood oozed from his lips. They raised his head and motioned to the Mexicans that now gathered round, for water; some was hastily procured, and then Mary entreated one of them to go for Dr. Bryant; as she spoke, the tramp of hoofs caused her to look up and she perceived him urging his horse toward them. He flung the reins to a man who stood near, and bent over the prostrate form.

" There is some internal injury, I see no outward wound; how did this happen ?"

Florence briefly explained the manner in which her father received a kick on the chest. Happily they were near their own home, and, with the assistance of two men, Dr. Bryant carefully bore him in and laid him on a couch near the open window. A restorative was administered, and soon the sufferer opened his eyes. The flow of blood had ceased, but he lay quite exhausted.

The physician examined the wounded place and assured Florence there was no fracture.

" I am afraid some blood-vessel is ruptured," said she anxiously.

" It is only a small one, I hope, but cannot tell certainly for several days. He must be perfectly quiet; the least excitement might prove fatal by causing a fresh hemorrhage."

Nearly a week passed, and one evening Mary followed the physician as he left the house; he heard her step and turned. His usually laughing countenance was grave and anxious; but he strove to seem cheerful.

"Doctor, I wish to know what you think of my uncle's case; we are afraid it is more serious than you at first pronounced it."

"It is better that you should know the worst. I am pained to grieve you, but candor compels me to say that a fatal injury has been inflicted. I hoped for the best, but an examination this evening confirmed my fears."

Mary sobbed bitterly and long. Dr. Bryant sought not to comfort her by exciting false hopes, but paced up and down the gravel-walk beside her.

"You do not fear a rapid termination of the disorder?" she said at last, in a low, trembling tone.

"He may linger some days, but I do not think it probable that he will."

"Florry, Florry! what is to become of us!" cried the weeping girl in a voice of agony. "Oh, God! spare him to us!"

"Do you think your cousin comprehends her father's danger?"

"She fears the worst and requested me this evening to ask your opinion. Oh, how can I tell her that he must die!"

"Do not crush all hope (though I have none); let her believe that he may recover. She is not of a temperament to bear prolonged agony. The shock will be less painful, rest assured. Believe me, I deeply sympathize with you both." And pressing her hand, he withdrew.

CHAPTER VIII.

"See! the dappled gray coursers of the morn
 Beat up the light with their bright silver hoofs,
 And chase it through the sky!"
—Marston.

INEZ left her father's door as the last notes of the matin bell died away on the cool, clear morning air. She held in her hand a silken scarf, which, according to the custom of her country, was thrown lightly across the head, and confined at the chin.

Beautiful she looked, with the feverish glow on her cheek, and her large Spanish eyes, restless and piercing, flashing out at times the thoughts of her inmost soul. She threw the mantilla round her head, and turned toward the church. The step was firm yet hasty. She seemed endeavoring to escape from herself.

The streets were silent, and the Plaza deserted, and naught seemed stirring save the swallows that twittered and circled round and round the belfry of the church. There was something soothing in the deep stillness that reigned on that balmy morning, and Inez felt its influence. She paused at the entrance of the gray old church, and stretched forth her arms to the rosy east.

" Peace, peace!" she murmured, in a weary tone, and sunk her head upon her bosom. The door opened behind her, and raising herself proudly, she drew the scarf closer about her, and entered.

A basin of holy water was placed near, and hastily she signed the figure of the cross, and proceeded down the aisle to a side door leading to one of the wings. She pushed it noiselessly ajar, and passed in.

A solitary tin sconce dimly lighted the small confessional, dark and gloomy as night, at that early hour. A wooden cross suspended from the wall, a stone bench and table, on which lay a rosary and crucifix, and a small vessel of holy water, formed the entire furniture. Before this table sat Father Mazzolin, his face buried in his hands. Her step, light as it was, startled him; yet without rising, he murmured, " Benedicit."

" Buenos dias, Padre."

He motioned to her to kneel, and she did so, on the damp floor at his feet, drawing the scarf over her face, so as to conceal the features.

" Bless me, my Father, because I have sinned."

He laid his hands on her bowed head, and muttered, indistinctly, a Latin phrase. " I confess to Almighty God, to blessed Mary, ever Virgin, to blessed Michael the Archangel, to blessed John the Baptist, to the holy apostles Peter and Paul, and to all the saints, that I have sinned exceedingly in thought, word, and deed, through my most grievous fault. Therefore I beseech the blessed Mary, ever Virgin, the blessed Michael the Archangel, the blessed John the Baptist, the holy apostles Peter and

Paul, and all the saints, to pray to the Lord our God for me.

"Since my last confession, I accuse myself of many sins. I have missed mass, vespers, and many holy ordinances of our most holy church. Have borne hatred, and given most provoking language.

"I have broken the engagement thou didst command me to keep; have angered Mañuel, and enraged my father greatly. I neglected fasting on the day of our most holy Saint——

"I have entered this church, this holy sanctuary, without crossing myself; and passed the image of the blessed Virgin without kneeling." She paused, and bent her head lower.

The Padre then said, "My daughter, thy sins are grievous; my heart bleeds over thy manifold transgressions."

"Even so, my Father; even so."

"Dost thou still bear enmity to Mañuel Nevarro, who loves thee truly, and is thy promised husband?"

"No, my Father; I desire to be speedily reconciled to him whom I have offended."

"Wilt thou promise to offer no objection, but become his wife?"

"My Father, I do not wish to be his wife; yet thy will, not mine."

A smile of triumph glittered in the Padre's eye at this confession; yet his low tone was unchanged.

"Inez, I will not force thee to marry Mañuel, yet thou shalt never be another's wife. In infancy thou wast promised, and thy hand can never be joined to another. Choose you, my daughter, and choose quickly."

"Padre, give me time. May one so guilty as I speak out?"

"Yes, speak; for I would have thine inmost thoughts."

"Father, let me spend a month of peace and quiet among the holy sisters at San Jose; there will I determine either to be Mañuel's wife, or dedicate the remainder of my life to the service of God and our most Holy Lady."

"You have spoken well; even so shall it be; but Inez, I would question you further, and see you answer me truly, as you desire the intercession of the blessed Virgin."

Inez lifted her head, and fixing her eyes full on his swarthy face, replied with energy:

"My father, even as I desire the intercession of our blessed Virgin, so will I answer."

The head was bent again on her bosom. He had sought to read her countenance during that brief glance, but there was a something in its dark depths he could not quite understand.

"My daughter, hast thou been of late with that Protestant girl, by name Mary Irving."

"I have seen her twice since last coufession."

"Where did you meet her?"

"Once at Señora Perraras, and once she came for me, to walk with her."

"Answer truly. Upon what subject did you converse?"

Inez seemed striving to recall some portion of what had passed. At last she said, "Indeed, Padre, I cannot remember much she said. It was mostly of birds, and trees, and flowers, and something, I believe, about this beautiful town, as she called it."

"Think again. Did she not speak lightly of the blessed church, and most holy faith? Did she not strive to turn you to her own cursed doctrines, and, above all, did she not speak of me, your Padre, with scorn?"

"No, my father, most truly she did not." Again she raised her eyes to his face. Piercing was the glance he bent upon her. Yet hers fell not beneath it: calm and immovable she seemed.

He lifted his hand menacingly.

"I bid you now beware of her and her friend, the trader's wife. They are infernal heretics, sent hither by the evil one to turn good Catholics from their duty. I say again, beware of them!" and he struck his hand heavily on the table beside him. "And now, my daughter, have you relieved your conscience of its burden? Remember, one sin withheld at confession will curse you on your death-bed, and send you, unshriven, to perdition!"

A sort of shudder ran through the bowed form of Inez, and in a low tone she replied, "I also accuse myself of all the sins that may have escaped my memory, and by which, as well as those I have confessed, I have offended Almighty God through my most grievous fault."

"I enjoin upon you as penance for the omission

of the holy ordinances of our most holy church, five Credos when you hear the matin bell, twelve Paters when noon comes round, and five Aves at vespers. These shall you repeat, kneeling upon the hard floor, with the crucifix before you and your rosary in your hand. In addition, you must repair to a cell of San Jose and there remain one month. Moreover, you shall see and speak to none save the holy sisters. And now, my daughter, I would absolve you."

Inez bent low while he spread his hands above her head and pronounced the Latin text to that effect, then bade her rise, and dismissed her with a blessing.

The sun was just visible over the eastern hills as Inez stepped upon the plaza. Her face was deadly pale and the black eyes glittered strangely.

"I have knelt to you for the last time, Father Mazzolin. Long enough you have crushed me to the earth; one short month of seeming servitude, and I am free. Think you I too can not see the gathering tempest? For long I have watched it rise. It may be that happiness is denied me; but yonder gurgling waters shall receive my body ere I become a lasting inmate of your gloomy cell. My plan works well; even my wily Padre thinks me penitent for the past! But dearly have I bought my safety. I have played false! lied! where is my conscience? Have I one? No, no! 'tis dead. Dead from the hour I listened to the Padre's teachings! If there be a hereafter, and, oh! if there is a God, what will become of me?" and the girl shuddered convulsively.

"Yet I have heard him lie. I know that even he heeds not the laws of his pretended God! He bade me follow his teachings, and I did and I deceived him! Ha! he thinks the game all at his fingers' ends. But I will neither marry Mañuel nor be a holy sister of Jose. There will come a time for me. Now I must work, keep him in the dark, spend the month in seclusion; by that time the troubles here will begin, and who may tell the issue?"

A quick step behind her caused Inez to turn in the midst of her soliloquy. Dr. Bryant was hastening by, but paused at sight of her face.

"Ah, Señorita! How do you do this beautiful morning?" He looked at her earnestly, and added: "You are too pale, Inez—much too pale. Your midnight vigils do not agree with you; believe me I speak seriously; you will undermine your health." Her eyes were fixed earnestly on his noble face, beaming with benevolence, and a slight flush tinged her cheek as she replied: "Dr. Bryant, I am not the devout Catholic you suppose me. The Padre thinks me remiss in many of my duties, and I am going for a short time to San Jose. You need not look at me so strangely, I have no idea of becoming a nun, I assure you."

"Inez, one of your faith can never be sure of any thing; let me entreat you not to go to the convent. You need recreation, and had much better mount your pony, and canter a couple of miles every morning; it would insure a more healthful state of both body and mind."

"I must go, Dr. Bryant."

"Well then, good-by, if you must, yet I fear you will not return looking any better."

"Adios," and they parted.

Inez's eye followed the retreating form till an adjoining corner intervened. Then pressing her hand on her heart, as if to still some exquisite pain, she murmured in saddened tones—"Oh! I would lay down my life for your love, yet it is lavished on one who has no heart to give in return. Oh, that I may one day be able to serve you!"

At that moment she perceived Mañuel Nevarro crossing the Plaza, and drawing closer the mantilla, she hastened homeward.

CHAPTER IX.

"A perfect woman, nobly planned;
To warn, to counsel, to command,
The reason firm, the temperate will,
Prudence, foresight, strength, and skill."
— *Wordsworth.*

THE beautiful ideal of Wordsworth seemed realized in Mrs. Carlton. She was by nature impetuous, and even irritable; but the careful training of her deeply pious mother early eradicated these seeds of discord and future misery. She reared her "in the way she should go," and taught her to "remember her Creator in the days of her youth." Crushing vanity, which soon rose hydra-headed in her path, she implanted in her daughter's heart a sense of her own unworthiness, and led her to the "fountain of light and strength."

Under her judicious care, Ellen's character was moulded into perfect beauty. She became a Christian, in the purest sense of the term. Hers were not the gloomy tenets of the anchorite, who with a sort of Spartan stoicism, severs every tie enjoined by his great Creator, bids adieu to all of joy that earth can give, and becomes a devotee at the shrine of some canonized son of earth, as full of imperfections as himself. Neither did she hold the lighter and equally dangerous creed of the latitudinarian. Her views were of a happy medium; liberal, yet perfectly orthodox.

Ellen married early in life, and many were the trials which rose up to test her fortitude, and even her reliance on Almighty God. Of six beautiful children that blessed her union, four went down to an early tomb. Though bowed to the earth by the weight of her affliction, she murmured not against the hand that chastened her; but as one by one was snatched from her warm embrace, she poured out the depth of a mother's love on the remaining two.

One stroke of fortune reduced her, in a day, from affluence to comparative penury; and leaving his luxurious home, Mr. Carlton resolved to seek his fortune in the Western World. Hither she had accompanied him, encountering, without a murmur, the numerous hardships, which those who have not endured can never fully realize. They had preceded Mr. Hamilton but a few months, and joyfully welcomed him as an agreeable acquisition to their little circle.

Mrs. Carlton found in Mary a real friend; one who sympathized with, and assisted her in her many benevolent plans for ameliorating the condition of the destitute Mexicans around them.

With Florence, the former had little affinity, and, consequently, little intercourse. Their tastes were directly opposite; and though they often met, there was no interchange of the deep and holier feelings of the heart.

Frank Bryant was the orphan-brother of Mrs. Carlton, and almost as dearly loved by her as her own darling Elliot. A few months before St. ——'s day, he reached San Antonio, on a visit to the sister, from whom he had been separated several years. Soon after his arrival, an epidemic made its appearance among the lower order of Mexicans; and as there was no resident physician at that early time, his services were speedily in requisition. The Padre, who numbered among his many acquirements a tolerable knowledge of medicine, viewed with indifference the suffering around him; and was only roused from his lethargy by discovering the flattering estimation in which Frank was held. Fearing so formidable a rival in the affections of his people, he left no means untried to undermine the popularity so deservedly acquired. But gratitude is a distinguishing trait of Indian character; and though apparently obeying the injunctions of their Padre, to follow no directions save his own, they reverenced Dr. Bryant as a being of superior order.

It was beside the bed of a dying friend that Inez first met him. One long, weary night they watched together, and when at last death freed the sufferer, with mingled emotions of admiration and gratitude she thanked him for the attentions conferred with such disinterested benevolence. She could not avoid contrasting the conduct of the cold and calculating Jesuit with the warm-hearted kindness of the noble stranger.

In a few days it became evident that she had herself imbibed the disease, and her terrified father besought the young physician to restore her. With unwearied patience he watched over the beautiful Señorita, whom Mrs. Carlton and Mary most carefully nursed, and was rewarded by the glow of returning health.

The idols of her youth were neglected and forgotten; one image filled Inez's heart, and before it she poured out all the passionate love of her ardent nature; hence her aversion to a union with Mañuel Nevarro.

Dr. Bryant early perceived her attachment; and knowing full well that he could never return it, avoided her society with a delicacy peculiarly his own. When thrown accidentally into her presence, his manner was frank, kind, and brotherly.

Inez did not deceive herself for a moment by supposing that he would ever return her love. She knew too well the nature of the barrier which intervened. To remain unfettered, to see, to love, and one day to serve him, was her dearest wish; and for its gratification she dared the rage of her father, and the hatred of her Padre. She fancied he loved another, and with the characteristic jealousy of her nation, an aversion to that object settled on her heart.

Dr. Bryant had nursed the last patient into convalescence: still he lingered, and at the close of St. ——'s day, announced his intention of remaining until the difficulties with Mexico were either amicably arranged, or war declared. Mary and Florence he often met, for he was a constant visitor at Mr. Hamilton's. His manner toward them was very different; with Mary he ever assumed the light bantering tone of brotherly freedom; with Florence he was always grave and earnest. Their conversation was generally upon literary topics, of which she was fond. Many were their discussions for and against their favorite authors and philosophers. In these arguments Mary seldom took part, though fully qualified to do so. Occasionally her cousin asked her opinion on various topics; at such times she gave them clearly, yet modestly, and with a gentle dignity peculiar to herself. The earnest attention with which Frank listened to her views, and his happy smile, when they coincided with his own, somewhat puzzled Mary; yet she welcomed his repartees with the same bright smile, and allowed distrust and jealousy no room in her heart.

CHAPTER X.

> "He swore that love of souls
> Alone had drawn him to the church; yet strewed
> The path that led to hell with tempting flowers,
> And in the ear of sinners, as they took
> The way of death, he whispered peace."
> —*Pollok.*

How wearily pass the hours to the anxious watcher beside the couch of pain. To her, it seems as though the current of time had forgotten to run on and join the mighty past, and that its swift waters were gathering glassily around her. With unmitigated care Florence had attended the bedside of her suffering parent; occasionally slumbering on his pillow, but more frequently watching through the long nights, and often stealing to the casement, to look out upon surrounding gloom, and wonder if the light of day would ever fall again on earth. Ah! in the midnight hour, when all nature is hushed, when universal darkness reigns, when the "still small voice" will no longer be silenced, then we are wont to commune with our own hearts. All barriers melt away, and the saddened past, the troubled present, and the shadowy future rise successively before us, and refuse to be put by. In vain we tightly close the aching lids; strange lurid lights flare around us, and mysterious forms glide to and fro.

To the guilty, how fearful must the season of darkness prove, when, unable longer to escape from themselves, they yield to the pangs of remorse, and toss in unutterable anguish !

"By night, an atheist half believes a God."

And thousands, who in the sunny light of day rush madly on to ruin, pause, shudderingly, in the midnight hour, and look yearningly toward the narrow path where Virtue's lamp, flashing into the deepest recesses of surrounding gloom, dispels all shadow; and, in imagination, view the Christian peacefully descending the hill of life, fearlessly crossing the " valley of the shadow of death," and resting at last on that blest shore, where night and darkness are unknown, " swallowed up in endless day."

It was very evident that Mr. Hamilton could survive but a few days; and to every entreaty that she would take some rest, Florence but shook her head, and replied, that she would not leave him when he must die so soon.

One evening Dr. Bryant, having administered a soothing potion, turned to her and said, " My dear Miss Hamilton, you will seriously injure your health by such constant watching. Your father needs nothing now but quiet. Let me entreat you to go out for a short time; the air will refresh you, and your aunt will remain with Mr. Hamilton." He drew her reluctantly from her seat as he spoke, and whispered Mary to accompany her.

Drawing her arm round Florence, Mary turned in the direction of their accustomed rambles, but her cousin said, " I am too weary to walk far, let us go to our old seat by the river."

The stream was only a few yards distant, and they seated themselves on a broad, flat stone, beneath a cluster of pomegranate and figs. The evening was beautifully clear, the soft light which still lingered in the west mellowing every object, and the balmy southern breeze, fresh from " old ocean's bosom," rustling musically amidst the branches above. As if to enhance the sweetness of the hour, and win the mourners from their sad thoughts, the soothing tones of the vesper-bells floated afar on the evening air; distance had softened them, and now they sounded clear and Eolian-like. The river eddied and curled rapidly along at their feet; and ever and anon, the stillness that seemed settling around was broken by the plunging fish that gamboled in hundreds amidst its blue waters.

"How calm and holy this stillness seems! Florry, does it not cause you to lift your heart in gratitude to the 'Almighty Giver' of so many blessings?"

" All things are dark to sorrow;" replied Florence, and folding her arms across her bosom, she dropped her head wearily upon them.

" Oh, Florry, do not give up so I can not bear to hear your despairing tone. Still hope; your dear father may be spared to us;" and she put her arms caressingly around her.

" Hope!" echoed Florence; " I have ceased to hope that he will recover. I know that he can not; and in a few hours I shall be alone in the world. Alone,

alone!" she repeated the words as if fully to realize the misery in store for her. "O God! why hast thou not taken me before? Take me now; oh, in mercy take me with him!"

In vain Mary strove to soothe and console her; she remained perfectly still, her face hid in her arms, and replied not to her anxious questionings. A long silence ensued, and Mary wept. A feeling of desolation began to creep over her; a second time she was to be thrown on the wide, cold world. She thought of her uncle's generosity and unvaried kindness during the many years she had dwelt under his roof, and scarcely felt that it was not her own. And then there stole up the image of her lost mother the wan, but saint-like face, and the heavenly smile with which she pointed upwards, and bade her child prepare for the glorious union, in that mansion which Jehovah assigned to those who are faithful on earth.

Poor Mary's heart was sad indeed; yet there was no bitterness in her soul, no rebellious feelings toward Almighty God, who had thus afflicted her so sorely. She wiped away her tears, and calming herself as much as possible, repeated in a faltering voice the beautiful hymn commencing " I would not live always." She paused at the conclusion of the second verse; but Florence did not lift her head, and hoping to cheer her, she finished the hymn.

Twilight had fallen on the earth, and the blue vault of heaven was studied with its myriad lamps. The new moon glittered like a golden thread—low in the west—and seemed almost to rest upon the bosom of the stream, as it curved in the distance to meet the horizon.

"Come, Florry, you must not stay out so late; I am afraid you will take cold!"

Florence rose mechanically and accompanied her.

"Oh, Florry, do try and trust in God, and believe that in every trial and affliction he will comfort and assist us."

Her cousin sighed heavily but made no reply.

As they reached the gate it was quickly opened, and the Padre met them; he bowed coldly to Mary, but shook hands with Florence, and promised to come again the ensuing day. It was so late that Mary could not distinguish his features; but just as he turned to go, Aunt Fanny threw open the kitchen door, and the light streamed full on his face; their eyes met, and she started at the smile of triumph that irradiated his dark countenance; he bowed and passed on.

Mary hastened down the walk and entered the sick room, fearing she scarcely knew what. The invalid was tossing restlessly from side to side, and on the pillow lay a rosary and crucifix. For an instant she stood motionless; then sprang forward, and clasped his burning hand in hers.

"Uncle! dear uncle! tell me who has been with you! Aunt Lizzy promised she would not leave you till we came back. You have been excited; your hands are burning with fever!"

"I was not alone, Mary; the Padre sat and talked

with me;" as the sufferer spoke, he shuddered and closed his eyes.

"And did he leave these here?" said she, taking up the crucifix and rosary.

"No, no! they are mine!" and he snatched them from her.

Mary turned pale, and leaned against the bed for support. Florence, now bending over her father, motioned to her cousin to be silent; without effect; however; for, passing round the bed, she knelt beside him. "Uncle, was it by your desire that the Padre came here this evening?"

He did not seem to hear her question; she repeated it.

"Yes; that is, this is not his first visit."

"Uncle, why do you evade me? Tell me, I entreat you, if he did not force himself here in my absence!"

"Mary, will you drive my father delirious with your interference with his wishes?"

"No, Florry, not when I am convinced that such are his wishes. I know that in health he is no more a Papist than you or I; yet now I see him clinging to that rosary and crucifix, what am I to think? If you can explain this mystery, do so, Florry."

"The day that you were at Mrs. Carlton's learning to make that custard my father likes so well, the Padre came and kindly sat with him some time. He came the next night, and the next; and read and prayed with him. I hope you are satisfied now that there is no intrusion." All this was whispered so low as not to reach the ears of the invalid.

"Were you present at any of these interviews, Florry?"

"No; they always preferred being alone."

"Oh! why did you not tell me this before?"

"I am sure I can't see what you are so excited about! If my father chooses to become a Catholic, I should think it would relieve you to know that he realizes his situation." She turned resolutely away as she finished speaking, and seated herself beside the bed.

Mary left the room almost stunned by the discovery she had made; and scarce knowing what to do, wrapped her shawl about her and walked quickly to Mrs. Carlton's. To her she related all she had just learned, and begged her advice and assistance.

Mrs. Carlton was sorely puzzled and much distressed.

"I fear, Mary, it is too late to remedy the evil."

"Oh, do not say so! I cannot bear that he should die in that faith; he is too feeble to oppose anything they offer, and is scarcely conscious of his own actions. In health, they dared not approach him; for they knew full well that he scorned their creed and disliked their Padre. Yet now that he is so weak, in both body and mind, they hope to influence him. Oh, how could Florence be so blind? Dear Mrs. Carleton, come and reason with him. I know he he esteems you very highly, and your opinion might weigh with him."

"Indeed, my dear child, I will do all in my power to dissuade him from the unfortunate course he has taken, but not to-night; he must be wearied very much already. I will come in the morning."

Early the ensuing day she fulfilled her promise, and in Florence's presence strove to elicit his views and belief. To her surprise he refused to hold any conversation on the subject; declaring that his mind was made up, and that he was determined to die a member of the holy Catholic Church.

Before she could frame a reply they were startled by the sound of a struggle at the door, and the next moment it was flung wide open and Father Mazzolin, livid with rage, rushed in. Mrs. Carlton rose with gentle dignity and inquired his business. He heeded not her question but strode to the bed and whispered in Mr. Hamilton's ear. The invalid, in a voice so feeble that it was scarce audible, requested them to leave him with the Padre for an hour, as he wished to converse with him alone. Mrs. Carleton perfectly well understood that he but repeated the priest's orders, and perceiving that nothing could now be effected, left the room accompanied by Florence. But Mary clung to the bed and refused to go.

"You have taken advantage of my uncle's weakness to force yourself where your presence is unwelcome, and I will not leave him when he is too weak to oppose your orders."

He strove to force her out but she clung firmly to the bed; and muttering an oath between his teeth, he turned to the sufferer and spoke in an unknown tongue; a feeble response in the same language seemed to satisfy him, and darting a triumphant glance at the kneeling girl, he seated himself and conversed for nearly an hour. Then offering up a Latin prayer, departed, promising to come again.

Mrs. Carlton had not left the house; she waited anxiously for Mary. And when Florence re-entered the sick-room, the former hastened to her friend.

"Oh, I did all I could to prevent it!" cried Mary, in despair. "All is over, I am afraid. I was sitting on the door step preparing some arrowroot, when I saw Aunt Lizzie go out the gate. I thought it strange at the time of day, but never suspected the truth. Presently I saw her coming back with the priest, and knew in an instant she had gone for him. I was determined to prevent his seeing my uncle if possible, and fastened the front door. Before I could lock my uncle's, he wrenched open the window and sprang in. I tried to put the key in my pocket and told him he could not go in then; but he made Aunt Lizzy hold one of my hands, while he forced open my fingers and took the key. Oh! that Dr. Bryant had been here." She showed Mrs. Carlton the marks of his grasp on her wrist. "Tell, oh, tell me what I can do to save him!"

"Alas! nothing, Mary. He is completely under the control of the Padre, and no reasoning will avail now."

With a sad heart Mrs. Carlton took leave, advising Mary "to offer no further resistance, as it was now impossible to convince her uncle of his error."

CHAPTER XI.

"He's gone—his soul hath ta'en its earthless flight,
Whither? I dread to think—but he is gone!"

Byron.

MR. HAMILTON, though perfectly conscious that his end was rapidly approaching, had scrupulously avoided the subject in the presence of the girls. One morning after a night of more than ordinary suffering, he lay quite exhausted. Death was at hand, and feeling intuitively that the appointed hour had arrived, he requested all to withdraw, save Florence. When they were alone he laid his hand on her head and said, in a low, feeble tone—" Florence, I am going. I cannot survive this day, and I wish to give you my last advice. I am afraid your lot will be a hard one when I am gone; trials without number are in store for you. Oh! my proud-hearted, beautiful Florence, what will become of you now?" He covered his face with his hands a moment, then continued—" I do not wish you to return to your native place. My child must be dependent on no one, yet to leave you here so unprotected, is hard indeed. Dr. Bryant has promised to watch over you, and the Carltons are kind friends. Florence, you must depend upon yourself. Thank God, you are strong-minded; and Mary, our kind, good Mary, will be near to comfort and assist you. I am growing weaker, but there is one more thing I wish to say."

He paused, and for the first time Florence spoke.

"My father, tell me every wish; fear nothing for me, there is nothing I can not bear now."

"For my sake, Florence, if not for your own, will you promise to be guided by Father Mazzolin?"

"Do you mean in matters of religion, my father?"

"I mean in all things; matters of interest as well as matters of faith. He will assist you much if you will but follow his advice and directions."

There was a pause, and then Florence said slowly, as if weighing every word—"Rest assured your wishes shall be my law. I will consult the Padre as you desire."

With a look of relief the dying man sank back on his pillow, and closed his eyes. Florence quickly summoned the physician and her aunt and cousin. A little while after, as Mr. Hamilton's eye fell on the weeping Mary, he extended his hand, and when she bent over him, drew her face down and imprinted a long kiss on her pale cheek. Even as he did so a dark form glided to the bedside. Another moment the uncle and niece were separated; none knew how, yet the Padre stood between, whispering low in the sufferer's ear. Almost gasping for breath, the latter intimated his desire to confess for the last time. And they were left alone.

Nearly an hour after the priest entered the apartment where Florence and Mary sat. He trembled visibly, yet, in his usual tone, said that he wished the family to be present at the last rites about to be performed for the dying Papist. They immediately repaired to the sick room, and the spectacle there presented made Mary quiver in every limb. The sufferer had been placed for convenience on a low couch, and was supported by pillows in an upright position. A dozen candles burnt around him, and a cloud of incense wreathed slowly along the wall. The room had been profusely sprinkled with holy water, and a chalice containing the consecrated wafer, sat near. Gasping for breath, Mr. Hamilton clasped a crucifix to his lips, though unable from weakness to secure it there; for twice it fell from his fingers and rolled to the floor.

Father Mazzolin, attired in a surplice ornamented with the insignia of his order, stood beside the bed, holding in one hand a superbly-bound volume—in the other a silver cup containing oil.

After a moment's pause he opened the book, and hurriedly read in a low, muttering tone, a Latin service of several pages. At the conclusion he carefully poured out a few drops of the oil, and just touched the palms of the sufferer's hands, and the soles of his feet, bidding him at the same time cross himself. Perceiving that he was utterly unable to do so, he hastily signed the figure and resumed his reading. How long he would have gabbled on, it is impossible to say, but a gasping sound from the dying man declared that dissolution was at hand, and snatching the chalice, he hastily administered the wafer, which was swallowed with difficulty. For the third time, Father Mazzolin strove to replace the crucifix in his hand and bend it to his lips. The cold fingers refused to clasp the consecrated wood, and sank, stiffened and powerless by his side.

Mary had gazed mournfully on as this mummery was enacted. A deathbed for a theatre, weeping relatives an audience, and Father Mazzolin an amateur performer. Aunt Lizzy was kneeling beside the Padre, ever and anon invoking the Virgin; while Florence sat with her face in her hands, almost as unconscious of what passed as her dying parent. She bent over him now, and in heart-rending accents conjured him not to leave her. He struggled in vain to utter words of comfort; they died away in whispers, and, with a slight moan, the spirit returned to the God that gave it. The Padre snatched his hat and hastily left the house, while Mary gave vent to an uncontrollable burst of sorrow. Florence seemed suddenly frozen, so rigid was her countenance as she gazed on the cold form below her. She neither wept nor moaned, but closed the eyes with a long, long kiss, and drawing a sheet over the marble features, turned with a slow, unfaltering step, away.

CHAPTER XII.

"For now that Hope's last ray is gone,
Sure Lethe's dream would bless:
In grief to think of bliss that's flown,
Adds pangs to wretchedness."
—*Anonymous.*

A FORTNIGHT had passed, and again it was evening. In the small dining-room of Florence Hamilton's humble home was assembled the now diminished family circle. Florence sat sadly apart, leaning her head, with closed eyes, against the window. The tea-bell rang; she lifted her head, glanced round the room, and wearily dropped her brow again on its resting place. Mary approached, and taking her hand, said in a gentle, winning tone, " Come, Florry dear."

" Eat your supper, Mary; I do not wish any."

" But you have not eaten anything to-day, and need something; do try, for my sake."

" I can not. If you knew how both head and heart ache, you would not urge me."

Mary turned away, and ate the usually joyous meal with a heavy heart. Florence had left her seat, and was standing in the door; as her cousin rose from the table she beckoned to her, and passed hurriedly out. Mary strove to catch her arm, but she hastened on as if trying to escape from herself.

Suddenly she paused by the river side, and clasped her hands convulsively over her head.

"Mary! Mary! you know not what I suffer."

"Florry, sit down, and lean your weary head on my shoulder."

She dipped her hand in the water, and dashed the cold, sparkling drops on her cousin's burning brow, speaking the while in a low, soothing tone. Florence rested a few moments in her cousin's arms, then threw herself on a grassy bank, and covered her face; one long, deep groan alone attesting her mental anguish. Mary wept more bitterly than she had yet done; still, she was so quiet, none would have known her grief, save from the tears that fell over her hand and arms. Can it be, that the spirits of departed friends hover near us while on earth, and draw closer in hours of woe? If so, why is it denied to the suffering one to hear again the dear accents of the "loved and lost?" Why may not their silver pinions fan the burning brow of sorrowing mortality, and the echo of Heaven's own melody murmur gently, "Peace, peace and joy for evermore?"

Florence stood up before her cousin; all trace of emotion had passed away, and left her calm. The bright moon shone full on her face. Oh! how changed since the morning she stood in Madame ———'s school-room. The large dark eyes were sunken; the broad brow marked with lines of mental anguish; the cheeks colorless, and her long, raven hair tossed back, and hanging like a vail below her slender waist. There was a hollow, wasted look in every feature; the expression was one of hopeless misery, and a something there was which made the heart ache, yet the haughty glance of other days might still be seen.

"Mary, look at me!"

"Well, Florry, I have looked at you, and sad enough it makes me feel."

"I am changed, Mary, strangely changed, am I not? Answer me truly."

"Yes, you look weary and ill; but why do you ask me such a question? You have had cause to look pale."

"Ah! you say truly; but, Mary, have you never suspected that a secret grief was freezing the life-blood in my cheeks?"

"Florry, what do you mean? I am afraid you are feverish!" and Mary laid her hand anxiously on her cousin's. It was flung contemptuously off.

"Mary, listen to what I have to say. I am in a strange mood to-night, and you must not contradict me. Where shall I begin? When my mother died I was four years old, they say, and a very delicate child. My mother! how strange it sounds. Yet I can at times faintly remember her beautiful face. Very faintly, as in a dream, I have seen an angel visitant. My mother, why did you leave your hapless babe? Oh! why? my mother! I was left much to myself, and followed unrestrained my own inclinations. You know my fondness for books; that fondness was imbibed in girlhood, as I wandered in my own sunny home—my lost home. My father taught me to conceal my emotions—to keep down the rising sob, to force back the glittering tear; and when I smiled over some childish grief, applauded my stoicism. I became unnatural, cold, haughty, but not unfeeling. I remember well how your pale face and mourning dress touched my heart, and waked my sympathies. From that hour I lavished my love on my father and yourself. Years passed and we went to New Orleans———" Here Florence paused, and closed her eyes for a moment, but quickly resumed—" You know how I studied. Mary, was it merely from love of metaphysics and philosophy, think you? No, no! Mr. Stewart's look of surprise and pleasure as, one by one, I mastered various intricacies, was the meed for which I toiled. Mary, from the first day we met, I loved him, for his was a master spirit. I worshiped him in my inmost soul, and he loved me in return. I know— I feel that he did. Yet he was even prouder than myself, and would have scorned to speak of love to one who never smiled in his presence. Oh! often when he stood beside my desk giving instruction, my heart has sprung to him. I have longed to hear the words of tenderness that welled up from his heart, but scorned to tremble on his lips. No look of love ever fell on me. His glance was cold and haughty. Oh, how inconsistent is woman! I yearned for his love; yet, had he tendered it, under my haughtiness would have dropped my idol—have shivered it at my feet. Weeks passed, and while near him I knew no sorrow; but the morning of my life was destined to be short. The cloud that had lowered on the horizon suddenly darkened around. That never-to-be-forgotten letter came, and I saw a great gulf open at my feet. An invisible hand placed Dudley Stewart on one brink, and I was left upon the other; and an unknown messenger thundered the decree of separation—' Forget the past and live again in the future!' I started as from a frightful dream. The cold reality forced itself upon me. Mary, a suspicion stole into my heart and stunned me. I thought for a brief time that Mr. Stewart loved you, and whose hand may register the darkened thoughts that crowded bitterly up? The morning we left New Orleans, I went into the school-room for our books. Ah! who may know the agony of that hour! I sat down in his chair, and laid my head on his desk, and groaned in mine anguish of spirit. Oh! Mary, that was the blackest, bitterest hour of my life. I had fancied he loved me; I feared I was deceived; I hated—despised myself for my weakness. Yet I could not reproach him; he had never sought my love.

" I had just risen from his desk when Mr. Stewart came in. He did not seem to see me, but took a seat near the door. I was well-nigh exhausted, but strove to appear as cold and indifferent as ever. I gathered up my books and turned to go, then he laid down his pen, and came to me.

" 'I believe you and your cousin leave to-day?'

" ' Yes, in this evening's boat,' I answered, much as usual.

"' I wish you a safe and pleasant voyage. My kindest adieux to your cousin. Good-by, Miss Hamilton.'

"He held out his hand. I said 'good-by' as clearly and coldly as himself. Our hands met but an instant. There was no pressure—no warmth, and then he opened the door for me to pass. As he did so, our eyes met; his glance was calm and cold, but his lips were firmly compressed. Had he looked sad, mournful, or tender, I should have passed out and triumphed; but my overtasked strength gave way; a cold shudder crept through my frame, and consciousness forsook me. I never fainted before or since. When I revived, I raised my head and looked about me. I was reclining on a couch; he kneeling beside me, calmly, as he would have stood in class. He held my hand, and pressed it warmly.

"'Are you better now, Florence?'

"'Oh, yes, thank you,' I said, and rose to my feet.

"He still held my hand. I withdrew it, and turned to the door. He placed himself before it, and said—'Florence, it was well done; you are an admirable dissembler, but I am not deceived. You love me, and have for long, yet I freely acknowledge your love can never exceed my own. I love you better than my life, though perfectly aware that we are now parted forever. I am a poor tutor, dependent on my daily exertions for subsistence; you the cherished daughter of a wealthy and ambitious parent.'

"He drew me to him, and imprinted a long kiss on my lips; then put me gently back, and left the room.

"I never saw him again, but did I doubt his love?

No, no! I would sooner doubt my own existence. We embarked, as you know, in the evening. That night was beautiful—just such a one as this—serene and heavenly. I stole out on deck when others slumbered, and for a long weary hour paced to and fro. There was a wild tumult in my soul which would not be stilled, and every restraining effort but fanned the flame that raged within. A never-to-be-forgotten contest was waged that night, and my heart was the arena. My guardian angel whispered low, 'Forget the past as a feverish dream; it is not well for thee; forget, forget!' But the heaven-born accents were suddenly drowned by the wild shriek of my dark destiny—' Of Lethe's waters thou shalt never taste! I have shattered the goblet at thy feet, and scattered the draught to the winds of heaven! Behold the apotheosis of thine idol! At this shrine shalt thou bow evermore—evermore!'

"A new impulse was implanted within me; and, impotent to resist, I was impelled onward, and onward, till a chasm yawned at my feet. Yet a moment I trembled on the brink, then plunged desperately forward. Mary, listen. I knelt on the damp, glistening deck, and implored Almighty God to register my words in heaven. In his awful name and presence, I solemnly swore to love Dudley Stewart alone—to be his wife, or go down to the tomb as Florence Hamilton. I rose up calm—the fierce warring was stilled. Yet it was not inward peace that succeeded. My fate was sealed—the last page of destiny transcribed.

" Time passed, oblivious of the darkened hours it bore on its broad bosom. Mary, I have watched for one loved form, and listened for that calm, proud step. I have loved, and trusted, and believed that we should meet again. Deluded Florence! a period is put to thy hopes and fears! Mary, he is married! All is over for me. The dull, heavy weight resting upon my heart will soon crush out the life spark, and lay low my proud head. Ah! my cousin, you weep. I wish that I could; but tears have been *too* often scornfully repulsed; they come not now at my call. Oh, Mary, I am weary, weary! I long for rest, even the rest of the dark, still tomb! I have no hope— no wish. I am passive now. At last nature has broken the bonds so long forced upon her, and the reaction is strong indeed. You ask how I received my information: ah! you need not doubt its authenticity. Aunt Lizzy and his mother were old friends, and she received a letter the day before my father died, announcing *his* approaching union with a beautiful cousin! I am deservedly punished; I worshiped the creature and forgot the God. I needed a desperate remedy, and it is administered."

As Florence concluded she leaned heavily against a tree, and raised her eyes to the jeweled vault above. Just then a dense black cloud, which had floated up from the west, passed directly over the moon, obscuring the silvery rays. She pointed to it, and said, in a low, mournful voice—" How typical of my life and heart; shut out from joy and hope in one brief hour, unlike it ever to be brightened again."

"Oh! Florry, dear Florry! turn to God for comfort and succor in this hour of need. He will enable you to bear this trial, and go steadily on in the path of duty."

"Mary, I have no incitement to exertion; nothing to anticipate. My future is blank and dreary. I know my lot in life; I have nothing to hope for."

"Not so, Florry. Your future life will be an active one. Are we not dependent on our exertions for subsistence? and does not our little school open to-morrow? Cheer up, darling! all may yet be bright. Bury the painful remembrances of the past; believe me, peace, if not joyousness, will surely follow the discharge of your duties."

"I can not forget the past. Had he sought my love, I could scorn him for his baseness; but it is not so. I almost wish it were. Yet I know and feel that he loves me; and oblivion of the past is as impossible for him as myself. I know not what strange impulse has induced me to tell you all this. I did it half unconsciously, hoping for relief by revealing that which has pressed so heavily on my heart. Mary, never speak to me of it again; and, above all, do not mention his name. It has passed my lips for the last time, and all shall be locked again within my own heart. We will open the school to-morrow; and may God help me! Mary, pray, oh, pray for me! I had no mother to teach me, and prayer is a stranger to my lips."

She walked hurriedly to the house, and shut herself within her own apartment.

CHAPTER XIII.

"Freedom calls you! Quick! be ready;
Think of what your sires have been:
Onward! onward! strong and steady,
Drive the tyrant to his den."
—*Percival.*

WHEN Iturbide attempted to free his oppressed countrymen from the crushing yoke of Spanish thralldom, Liberty was the watchword. Success crowned his efforts—sovereign power lay before him. He grasped it, and made himself a despot. Ambition hurled him from the throne of the Montezumas, and laid his proud head low. A new star rose on the stormy horizon of the west; pure and softly fell the rays on the troubled thousands round. The voice of the new comer said " Peace," and the wild tumult subsided. Ten years passed: Santa Anna culminated. The gentle tones of the arch deceiver were metamorphosed into the tiger's growl, the constitution of 1824 subverted in a day, and he ruled in the room of the lost Iturbide.

* * * * *

The Alamo was garrisoned. Dark bodies of Mexican troops moved heavily to and fro, and cannon bristled from the embrasures. The usually quiet town was metamorphosed into a scene of riot and clamor; and fandangos, at which Bacchus rather than Terpsichore presided, often welcomed the new-born day. The few Americans* in San Antonio viewed with darkened brows the insolent cavaliers. The gauntlet was flung down—there was no retraction, no retreat. They knew that it was so, and girded themselves for a desperate conflict.

The declaration of independence was enthusiastically hailed by the brave-hearted Texans, as they sprang with one impulse to support the new-born banner that floated so majestically over the sunny prairies of their western home. Mechanic, statesman, plowboy, poet, pressed forward to the ranks, emulous of priority alone. A small but intrepid band, they defied the tyrant who had subverted the liberties of his country; defied Santa Anna and his fierce legions, and spurned the iron yoke which the priests of Mexico vainly strove to plant upon their necks. Liberty, civil and religious, was the watchword, and desperately they must struggle in the coming strife.

Mañuel Nevarro had eagerly enlisted in the Mexican ranks, and in a few weeks after General Cos's arrival, donned his uniform. Thus accoutred, he presented himself for the first time since their disagreement, before Inez, who had but recently returned from San Jose, doubting not that her admiration of

---

* It doubtless appears absurd to confine the title of "Americans" to the few citizens of the United States who emigrated to Texas, when all who inhabit the continent are equally entitled to the appellation. Yet the distinction is Mexican; "Los Americanos" being the name applied to all who are not of Spanish descent.

his new dress would extend to him who filled it. In truth, his was a fine form and handsome face; yet sordid selfishness, and, in common parlance, " a determination to have his own way," were indelibly stamped upon his countenance.

Inez was busily preparing the evening meal when he entered; and though perfectly aware of his presence, gave no indication of it. He stood aside and watched her movements as she shaped and turned the tortillas. Presently she began to sing

> "He quits his mule, and mounts his horse,
> And through the streets directs his course—
> Through the streets of Gacatin,
> To the Alhambra spurring in,
> Wo is me, Alhama.
>
> "And when the hollow drums of war
> Beat the loud alarm afar,
> That the Moors of town and plain
> Might answer to the martial strain,
> Wo is me, Alhama."

As the mournful cadence died away, she turned and started with well-feigned surprise on meeting the piercing glance fixed upon her.

"Ah, Mañuel!" She held out both hands, with a most amicable expression of countenance. He grasped them, and would have kissed her beautiful lips, but she slipped adroitly to one side—" No, no! Mañuel. I'll not permit that till I am Señora Nevarro."

"And when will that be, Señorita?"

"Not till the war is over."

"But it has not begun yet: and it will be many moons before we whip these cursed Americanos."

"How many, think you, Mañuel?"

"I can't tell, Inez; therefore we will not wait till the war is over. The Padre is ready any time, and why not marry at once?"

"Sacra Dios! I'll do no such thing."

"And why not, Inez?"

"Because they might kill you, Mañuel, and then what would become of me?"

"You would be as well off then as now; there would be no difference, only you would be married. You will mourn any how, if I am killed."

"How do you know I would?" Her Spanish eyes twinkled as she spoke; but for fear of going too far, she laid her hand on his shoulder. Mañuel turned sharply round.

"You deserve to be shot, Mañuel, for joining in a miff. Why didn't you tell me you were going to be a soldier?"

He grasped her hand tighter, but made no reply.

"I say, why did not you tell me first?"

"And if I had told you, what then?"

"Why I should not have let you do it, you savage. If you had only asked me, I might be willing to marry you next week. But as it is, I am not going to be left a widow, I can tell you."

"Inez, I don't believe you care whether I am killed or not. I do not understand you at all."

The girl's eyes filled, and her lip quivered with emotion. "Mañuel, do you think me a brute? There is nobody to love Inez but her father and you. I am not cold hearted."

"You speak truth, Inez; and my uncle will not live very long, for he has seen many years. When he is gone, there will be nobody to take care of you but me; so the sooner we are married the better."

"Not so. You must come and see us as often as you can till the war is over; but I will marry no one now."

"Will you promise it shall be as soon as the war is over?"

Inez coquettishly tossed her beautiful head, and advancing to the fire, gayly exclaimed—" While we talked the tortillas burned. Come, eat some supper. I know they are as good as those you get at the Alamo."

Mañuel seated himself on a buffalo-robe, and while partaking of the evening meal, Inez chatted away on indifferent subjects, asking, during the conversation what news had been received from the Texan army.

"We got news to-day that they are marching down to Gonzales, but I am thinking they will find hot work."

"How many men may we number, Mañuel, and think you the chances are for us?"

"By the blessed Virgin, if we were not ten to five, Mañuel Nevarro would not eat this tortilla in peace. The Captain says we will scatter them like pecans in a high wind."

"What bone is there to fight for at Gonzales?"

"Cannon, Inez, cannon. Don't you know we sent a thousand men to bring it here, and the white rascal sent five hundred to keep it there. By the Virgin, we will see who gets it!"

"Holy Mother protect us! Mañuel, take care of yourself, man, and rush not into danger. It will profit you little that we have many men, if some strong arm tells your length on the sward."

"Never fear, Inez—never fear. We must not stop till every American turns his back on the Alamo, and his face to the East."

"But you will not harm those that live here in peace with all men?"

"The Padre told our General yesterday, that we must fight till all submitted, or the last American child was driven to the far bank of the Sabine."

Inez laid her hand on his arm, and looking him full in the face, asked, in a low tow—"Mañuel, would you help to drive Mary from her home among us? She who nursed me in sickness, and bound the white bread to your bleeding arm, and made the tea for my dying mother, when none other came to help? Mañuel! Mañuel! she is alone in the world, with only her cousin. Spare Mary in her little home; she hurts none, but makes many to die in peace."

Mañuel's face softened somewhat, but he replied in the same determined tone—"The Padre says she is an accursed heretic, and he will not rest till she is far away. But I tell you now, Inez, she will not be harmed; for he said he would see that she was protected, and would himself take her to a place of safety. He said she had been kind to our people, and none should molest her or her cousin; but leave all to him."

"If the Padre promised, he will place them in safety; he never forgets to do what he says. I am satisfied, Mañuel; and for the rest of the Americans, the sooner they are driven out the better."

"You say truly, Inez, the sooner the better: all, all shall go, even their Doctor, that carries himself with such a lordly air, and sits in saddle as though never man had horse before. But the moon is up; I must return, for I watch to-night, and must be back in time." He put on his hat as he spoke.

"Mañuel, come as often as you can, and let me know what is going on. You are the only one whose word I believe; there are so many strange tales nowadays, I put little faith in any. And before you go, put this crucifix about your neck: 'twill save you in time of danger, and think of Inez when you see it." She undid the fastening which held it round her own throat, and pressing it to her lips, laid it in his hand.

Astonished at a proof of tenderness so unexpected, Mañuel caught her in his arms, but disengaging herself, she shook her finger threateningly at him, and pointed to the door. He lighted his cigarrita, and promising to come often, returned to the Alamo.

Left alone, the Spanish maiden sought her own

apartment, muttering as she ascended the steps—
"The Padre protect you, Mary? Yes, even as the
hawk the new chicken. Take you to a place of
safety! even as the eagle bears the young lamb to
his eyrie. Yes, Mañuel, I have bound the handkerchief about your eyes. You think I love you, and
trust both Padre and crucifix! Trust on, I too have
been deceived."

CHAPTER XIV.

MORE like somnambulism than walking reality was
now the life of Florence Hamilton. No duty was
unperformed, no exertion spared to conduce to the
comfort of the now diminished family circle. No
words of repining or regret were uttered—no tear
dimmed the large dark eyes. She moved and lived
as it were mechanically, without the agency of feeling or sympathy; yet though she obtruded her grief
on none, it was equally true that no gleam of returning cheerfulness ever lightened the gloom which
enveloped her. A something there was in the hopeless, joyless expression of her beautiful face which
made the heart ache; yet none offered sympathy or
strove to console her, for she seemed unapproachable with the cold, haughty glance of other days.
Painfully perceptible was the difference between
Christian fortitude and perfect hopelessness—gentle,

humble resignation and despair. There was no peace in her soul, for her future was shrouded in gloom; she had no joys in anticipation. The sun of hope had set forever to her vision, and she lived and bore her grief like one who had counted the cost and knew that for a little while longer she must struggle on; and that oblivion of the past was dispensed only by the angel of death. She acquiesced in Mary's plan of opening a small school, and unfalteringly performed her allotted tasks as assistant teacher. Unexpected success had crowned their efforts, and fifteen pupils daily assembled in the room set apart for the purpose. Mary had feared opposition on the part of the Padre, and was agreeably surprised at the number of Catholic children committed to her care.

One morning early in October, having finished her household duties, she repaired to the school-room for the day. Florence was already at her post, though suffering from violent nervous headache. Mary seated herself with her back to the door and called one of her classes—arithmetic it proved; and if the spirits of the departed were ever allowed to return in vindication of their works, the ghost of Pythagoras would certainly have disturbed the equanimity of the " muchachos," who so obstinately refused the assistance and co-operation of his rules and tables. In vain she strove to impress on one that 2 from 8 left 6. Like the little girl that Wordsworth met, he persisted " it was seven." Despairing at last, she remanded the class to their seats. Anxious to facilitate the progress of her pupils, Mary spared no pains to make perspicuous what to them appeared obscure. The little savages could not or would not understand that the earth was like a ball, and not only turned upon its own axis, but made the entire cirumference of the sun. A pair of globes could not be procured, and she taxed her ingenuity for a substitute; selecting two apples, one enormous, the other medium size, she carefully introduced a reed through the centre of the smaller apple, thus causing it to revolve on its axis. Calling up the tyros in geography, she took the smallest apple, or "Earth," as she designated it, and while causing it to perform the diurnal motion, she carried it slowly round the larger, or "Sun," as she termed it: thus illustrating the combined movements of our globe. Even the dullest could not fail to comprehend; and well satisfied with the result of her experiment, she carefully put her planets by in one corner of the school-room and proceeded with her questions. The imperfect recitation finished, Mary glanced across the room, hoping her cousin's patience was not so tried, and some brilliant coruscations in that direction fixed her attention. Florence had dropped her aching head on the desk in front, shading her eyes with her hand; before her, in dark array, stood some half dozen small boys just begining to spell. Each held a book containing illustrations of various well-known articles and animals having the name beneath.

"U-r-n—teapot." Elliot Carlton, whose seat was near, gave a suppressed giggle; Florence looked around inquiringly, then dropped her head again on her hand, bidding the boy "spell on."

"S-t-a-g—goat." Elliot Carlton crammed his handkerchief into his mouth and Mary smiled.

"W-i-g—curly head." Florence was effectually roused this time by a shout of laughter from Elliot, in which he was joined by Mary and Dr. Bryant, who had just entered and was standing in such a position that no one had perceived him.

"Really, Miss Hamilton, I must congratulate you on the extraordinary progress your pupils make; I was not aware that you cultivated their powers of comparison in connection with the rudiments of orthoepy."

"To what do you allude, Doctor; I am scarcely conscious of what passes around me this morning," said Florence, wearily pressing her hand across her aching brow.

"I am not surprised that you are somewhat stunned, though, after all," he continued, pointing to the picture of a ringleted pate, "the little fellow was not far wrong, for this wig is incontestibly a curly head."

With a faint smile, which passed as quickly as it came, she dismissed the class with an additional lesson.

"I am sorry to see you suffering so much this morning," said Frank, seating himself beside her; "and should certainly not recommend this school-room as an antidote to nervous attacks. Miss Mary, why do you allow your cousin to overtax her strength?

However, I bring you good news. We have had an engagment at Gonzales, and, thank Heaven, are victorious. The brave five hundred sent to preserve the field-piece there, encountered double their number of the enemy, and not only saved the cannon but scattered the Mexicans in all directions. Our brave band are marching to Goliad, where they expect to supply themselves and comrades with ammunition; they have probably taken the magazine before this and are returning."

"Thank Heaven we have triumphed!" cried Mary, fervently clasping her hands; "but oh! if the tide should turn this way, what will become of us? The Mexicans are numerous here, and the Alamo strongly fortified and in their possession." She turned her eyes inquiringly on Frank, and started as she met the earnest, searching expression of his, bent full upon her face.

"How pale you have grown of late," he murmured as to himself, and replied to her questioning glance —"I think, myself, there is much danger incurred by remaining here; but rest assured you shall not be harmed. I am watching the signs of the times, and will warn you should peril approach."

He took Florence's hand, and pressed it as he spoke; then turning to Mary, who had walked away, he said: "I must insist on your cousin having rest; she is weary and too much excited, and you, who are a good nurse, must take better care of her."

"Indeed, Doctor, I did my best to prevent her

teaching to-day, but she would not listen to my entreaties," replied Mary with averted head.

"If I might venture to advise yourself and cousin, Miss Hamilton, I should suggest the discontinuance of your school, at least for the present; for in these stormy times one scarce knows what a day may bring forth; and, indeed, your pupils are dropping off within the last few days, and you had better disband voluntarily."

"I believe you are right, Doctor; and if Mary concurs with us, I think we will follow your advice."

"Do as you think best, Florry; I suppose we would have no pupils soon, even if we continued our efforts! yet I dislike very much to give up the school so very soon." Her voice faltered slightly and her cheek grew paler.

"Your reluctance to dismiss these children, I am not surprised at; and if it will relieve you in the least, allow me to see their parents and arrange all pecuniary matters. You certainly feel no hesitation in confiding this to me."

"Thank you, Dr. Bryant, you are very kind; but we will not burden you with an additional trouble. I prefer taking these children home to their parents who committed them to my care; and as you and Florry think it advisable, we will close our school this evening. Believe me, however, that in refusing your kind offer, I am not insensible to, but appreciate fully, the motives which dictated it."

"Feel no hesitation in calling on me to perform any of the many services a gentleman friend may so often render. If you knew how gladly I would serve you, I am sure you would not fail to do so."

Shaking hands with Florence who stood near, he turned to go, but paused at the threshold.

At this moment a slight disturbance in a distant corner of the room attracted their attention, and springing forward, little Maria Carlton exclaimed—"Oh, Miss Mary, what do you think? Somebody has eat up the world, and bit a great big piece out of the sun!"

When the merriment this excited had in some degree subsided, Dr. Bryant laughingly said—"I am much afraid you have a Polyphemus among your pupils. Miss Mary, do discover the incipient monster, and eject him forthwith. Heavens, what powers of digestion he must possess! Good-morning, ladies—good-morning." And with a bow he left the house.

"Florry, dear, do try and sleep some! I will do all that is necessary about the children. True, there is not enough to occupy me long, and meanwhile you must impart the news of this victory to Aunt Lizzy."

CHAPTER XV.

"————I might not this believe
Without the sensible and true avouch
Of mine own eyes."
—*Shakespeare.*

TWILIGHT had fallen slowly, for the evening was heavy and wet, and dark masses of cloud driven by the northern blasts sailed gloomily overhead. Nature wore a dreary aspect, and one involuntarily turned inward for amusement. A bright light gleamed from the window of Florence Hamilton's humble home, and her little dining-room seemed by contrast extremely cheerful; yet the hearts of its inmates were more in accordance with the gloom which reigned without. Aunt Lizzy, growing somewhat infirm of late, had retired earlier than usual. Florence had been sewing all the afternoon, but now lay with closed eyes on the couch, her hands clasped over her head. Mary sat near the table holding an open volume, but her thoughts had evidently wandered far away! for her gaze was fixed abstractedly on the fire which blazed and crackled at her feet. The girl's countenance was an interesting study as she sat wrapped in her saddened thoughts. A care-worn expression rested upon her face, as though some weighty responsibility too soon had fallen on one so frail. The cheeks were very pale, and now and then across the lips there came a quiver, as though she struggled inwardly, and fain would give no outward show of grief. In truth, an almost spiritual expression had come over her features; the impress of some deep and hidden sorrow, nobly borne, though chasing the rosy hue from her cheeks. Sadder grew the look, and some acute pain wrinkled her brow as she threw aside the book and covered her face with her hands; while a heavy yet smothered sigh struggled forth, as if striving to relieve the aching heart.

The door opened noiselessly, and a dark shrouded form glided with soft steps to the chair, and laid a heavy hand on her shoulder. Mary raised her head and starting up, gazed inquiringly at the muffled face, while the intruder pointed to the motionless form of Florence, and laid a finger on her lip. Then beckoning Mary to follow, she receded with stealthy tread to the door which was softly closed, and walked hurriedly on till she reached a large rose-tree which shaded the window. Mary shivered as the piercing wind swept over her, and strove in vain to suppress a fit of coughing. There was a moment's silence.

"You did not know me?"

Mary started. "I did not, till you spoke; but, Inez, what brings you out on such a night?"

Inez took off the mantilla which had so effectually concealed her features and threw it round the frail, drooping form before her.

"No, no, Inez, you will take cold;" and Mary tendered it back.

It was tossed off contemptuously, and mingled with a bitter laugh came the reply—"I am not cold,

Mariñita, nor ever shall be but once again. I am burning with an inward fire that will not be quenched."

"You are ill, Inez, and want some medicine; tell me where and how you suffer."

"No, no. I want nothing from you or yours: I come to help, not to ask. Mary, why is it you have made me love you so, when I hate yonder dark-eyed girl? But I am losing time. I come to warn you of danger, and even now I am watched; but no matter, listen to what I have to say. The Padre hates you, even as—as I hate him, and has sworn your ruin. I tell you now you must fly from San Antonio, and fly quickly, for danger is at hand. My countrymen are many here, and he is stronger than all. You and I have thwarted him, and the walls of a far off convent are our destination—you, and your cousin, and myself. I am at heart no Catholic; I have seen the devil, if there be one, in my confessor. I have heard him lie, and seen him take the widow's and the orphan's portion. Mary, if there was a God, would he suffer such as my Padre to minister in his holy place, and touch the consecrated vessels? No, no; there is none, or he would be cut off from the face of the earth."

"Inez! Inez! stop and hear me."

"No, no! time waits for none, and I have little more to say. Mary, you are deceived; your cousin is not what you think. She is a Catholic; for mine own eyes have seen her in the confessional, and my own ears have listened to her aves and paters."

Mary uttered a deep groan, and clasped Inez's arm murmuring—"You are—you must be delirious or mad: Florry deceive me! impossible!"

"Ah! poor deluded Mary: do you trust any on earth? Yet I would trust you, with your white face and soft blue eyes; and there is one other I would trust—but no more. You will not believe that Florence has turned from the faith of her fathers? Go to her as she sleeps yonder, and feel with your own hand the crucifix around her neck. Ha! you hold tight to my arm: I tell you your Cousin Florence is as black-hearted as the Padre, for he told me she had promised her dying father to follow his advice in all things, yet she tells you not of this: and again, has she not won the love of a good, a noble man, and does she not scorn his love; else why is his cheek pale, and his proud step slow? Mariñita, I have read you long ago. You love your Doctor, but he loves that Florence, whose heart is black and cold as this night. You are moaning in your agony; but all must suffer. I have suffered more than you; I shall always suffer. My stream of bitterness is inexhaustible; daily I am forced to quaff the black, burning waters. Ha! I know my lot—I swallow and murmur not. Mary, I am sorry to make you drink so much that is bitter to-night; but you must, for your own good; better a friend should hold the cup and let you taste, than have it rudely forced upon you."

"Why have you told me this, Inez? I never did you harm, nor gave you pain."

"Poor pale face! I want to save you from worse than death—yea, from a living death. Go from this place: for if you are here a month hence, you will be lost. Your people here will be defeated, and then the Mexicans will hand you all over to the Padre, who says he means to put you where you will be protected. Mark me: you will be sent where no cry for succor will ever be heard. You will be imprisoned for life, where none can come back to tell the tale. Mary, go to your friends in the States; or if you can not get there, go where your people are many, and take your Doctor with you, for blood will yet run down these streets, and I would not that his swelled the stream. He has promised to watch over you; tell him to take you from here—from this cursed place. I have crept from home this dark night to tell you of your danger; I am watched, for the Padre suspects me, but you were always good; you nursed me and my dying mother, and were kind to Mañuel, and I would risk more than I have to help you. I have done all I can; I charge you, wait not till the last moment."

Inez stretched out her hand for her mantilla, which she folded closely about her face, and then clasped Mary's hand in hers.

"Inez! oh, Inez!"

"Well, Mariñita, I may not linger here. I will see you again if I can; but if we meet no more, forget not Inez de Garcia, or the love she bears you; and as the greatest blessing now for you, I hope you may soon find peace in the quiet grave. I shall never find rest till I sleep that last, unbroken sleep!"

"Inez, my heart is wrung by what I have heard to-night; but I beg of you, as a last favor, do not, oh, do not turn away from God! Inez, there is a God; and death is not an everlasting sleep. Hereafter is an awful tribunal; and if not again on earth, you and I shall assuredly meet before God. Oh! believe that he will yet bless you: that he will enable you to bear all earthly trials; and, if faithful, he will receive you at last into the kingdom of eternal rest. Try to forget the past, and in this book you will find the path of duty so clearly marked out, that you can not mistake it. 'Tis all I have about me, yet I pray God it may be the greatest treasure you possess."

She drew a small Bible from her pocket as she spoke, and pressed it within Inez's fingers, adding —" I can not sufficiently thank you for your kindness in warning me of my danger; I shall leave this place as soon as possible, and shall constantly pray that you may be spared and blessed."

She held out her hands. Inez clasped them tightly for a moment, and then glided down the walk as noiselessly as she came.

CHAPTER XVI.

"Be sure that you teach nothing to the people but what is certainly to be found in Scripture."
—*Bishop Taylor.*

MARY IRVING sought her chamber, and sinking on her knees, fervently implored the blessing and guidance of Him who is very precious help in time of need. She prayed for strength to meet with Christian fortitude the trials which awaited her, and in all the vicissitudes of her checkered life to pursue unfalteringly the path of duty. She strove to collect her scattered thoughts, and with what composure she could assume, returned to the dining-room. The fire was burning low on the hearth, and the single candle gave but a faint, unsteady light. Florence was slowly pacing up and down the floor; she raised her head as Mary entered, then sunk it wearily on her bosom and resumed her walk.

"Florry, come sit here by me—I want to consult you."

"Is it very important, Mary? I feel to-night as though I could comprehend nothing; let me wear off this dull pain in my heart and head by walking, if possible."

"My dear Florry, it is important; and therefore you will forgive me if I claim your attention."

Florence seated herself, and as she did so, leaned her head on Mary's shoulder, while the latter wound her arm fondly about her, and gently stroked back the raven hair from her aching brow.

"Since we broke up our school, I have been warned that we are in danger, and advised to leave San Antonio as speedily as possible; for strife is evidently at hand, and a battle-ground is no place for those so unprotected as you and I."

"Dr. Bryant has promised to watch over us; and surely you have implicit confidence in both his judgment and honor. What do you fear, Mary?"

"Every thing. We may remain here too long—till escape will be impossible; and then who may predict with any degree of certainty the chances of war? That Dr. Bryant will do all that a friend or brother would, I doubt not; but he may be powerless to help when danger assails; and even if he should not, to travel from here in stormy times would not be so easy as you imagine."

"Who has been filling your head with such ideas? It could be none other than that dark-browed Inez."

"If she has, could aught but disinterested friendship actuate her to such a course?"

"Really, Mary, I should not have given you credit for so much credulity. Do you place any confidence in what that girl may tell you?"

"I do rely on what she confides to me. Has she ever given you cause to doubt her sincerity? Indeed, Florry, you do her injustice. I would willingly—God only knows how willingly—doubt some portions of what I have heard from her lips, but I dare not."

"Mary, can you not perceive that she is jealous of us and hopes by operating on your fears, to drive us from this place? The Padre hinted as much to me not long since."

"Florry, it is for you to say whether Inez speaks truth. From her lips I had the words—Your cousin Florence is a Papist, wears a crucifix about her neck, and kneels in the confessional. Oh, Florry! will you —can you—do you deny the charge?"

The cousins stood up, and each gazed full upon the other. Mary's face was colorless as marble, and her hands were tightly clasped as she bent forward with a longing, searching, eager look. A crimson glow rushed to Florence's very temples; then receded, leaving an ashy paleness.

"I am a member of the Church of Rome."

Mary groaned and sank back into her chair, at this confirmation of her fears. Florence leaned against the chimney and continued in a low, but clear voice—"I have little to say in defense of what you may consider a deception. I deny the right of any on earth to question my motives or actions; yet I would not that you, Mary, who have loved me so long and truly, should be alienated without hearing the reasons which I have to allege in favor of my conduct. Mary, think well when I ask you what prospect of happiness there was for me a month since? Alone in the wide world, with ruined hopes and a long, long, joyless future stretching gloomily before me. I was weary of life. I longed for death, not as a passport to the joys of heaven (for

I had never sought or deserved them), but as bringing rest, peace, and oblivion of the past. I viewed it only as a long, last, dreamless sleep. Mary, I was groping my way in what seemed endless night, when suddenly there came a glimmer of light, faint as the first trembling rays of the evening star, and just pierced the darkness in which I wandered. The Padre came to me, and pointed to the long-forgotten God, and bade me seek him who hath said, ' Come unto me all ye who are weary, and I will give you rest.' Mary, do you wonder that I clasped the hand outstretched to save me, and besought him to lead me to the outraged and insulted God? My eyes were opened, and looking down the long, dark vista of the past, I saw how, worshiping a creature, I built a great barrier between myself and heaven. I saw my danger, and resolved, ere it was too late, to dedicate the remainder of my life to him who gave it. The door of the church was opened, and Father Mazzolin pointed out the way by which I might be saved. The paths seem flowery, and he tells me the ways are those of pleasantness and peace, and I have resolved to try them. Once, and once only, I met him at confession, hoping, by unvailing my sufferings to a man of God, to receive comfort of a higher order than I might otherwise expect. He has granted me absolution for the past, and I doubt not that in future the intercession of the blessed saints in heaven will avail with my offended Maker."

"Florry, my own dear Florry! hear me, for none

on earth loves you as I do. Do you not believe the Bible—God's written word? Has he not said, ' there is *one mediator* between God and man—the man Christ Jesus?' Has not Christ made propitiation for our sin, and assured us there is but one way whereby we may be saved, repentance for our past sins and faith in the sufficiency of his atonement? Do you doubt the efficacy of Christ's suffering and death? Tell me, Florry, by what authority you invoke your saints? Surely you do so in opposition to the express declaration of the Bible already quoted—' there is *one mediator* between God and man.'"

" The holy Fathers of our church have been in the habit of praying for the intercession of saints from the earliest periods, and none have questioned their fervent piety, or doubted the orthodoxy of their faith," replied Florence.

" In the first place," said Mary, " it would be ridiculous in the extreme to advocate all the opinions and tenets advanced by those same Fathers. St. Augustine doubted the existence of the antipodes; Tertullian emphatically pronounced second marriages adultery; Origen denied the sin of David in causing the death of Uriah, and has often been accused of favoring Arianism, and the doctrine of transmigration of soul; while it is a well-known fact that Jerome, to vindicate Peter from the charge of dissimulation, actually accused St. Paul of lying, and thereby favoring deceit. In the second place, are you quite sure that they were in the habit of invoking saints?"

"Certainly, Mary; for it is undeniable that St. Augustine in his Meditations calls on the blessed Virgin, and all the angels and apostles in heaven to intercede with God in his behalf. Father Mazzolin pointed out the passage no later than last week to remove the doubts which I confess I entertained, as to whether it was proper and in accordance with the practice of the Fathers to implore such intercession."

"And does your conviction rest on so frail a basis? Here what the Rev. Dr. Milner says on this subject in the first volume of his Ecclesiastical History;" and taking it from the shelf, Mary read:

"'The book of Meditations, though more known to English readers than any other of the works ascribed to Augustine, on account of the translation of it into our language by Stanhope, seems not to be his, both on account of its style, which is sententious, concise, abrupt, and void of any of those classical elegancies which now and then appear in our author's genuine writings; and also, on account of the prayers to deceased saints which it contains. This last circumstance peculiarly marks it to have been of a later date than the age of Augustine. Frauds of this kind were commonly practiced on the works of the Fathers in the monastic times.'

"And why, Florry, does it peculiarly mark it as spurious? Because, had he entertained these views on so vital a point, the expression of them would most certainly have occurred in his other very voluminous works. I have searched his Confessions for instances of this invocation, either from himself or anxious mother, and had he believed as the Catholic prelates assert, in this intercession of the dead, it would most assuredly have been sought in the hour of his suffering and fear, lest he should be given over. But I find none. On the contrary, these two passages occur in his Confessions: 'I now sought the way of obtaining strength to enjoy thee, and found it not, till I embraced the mediator between God and man, Jesus Christ, who is above all, God, blessed for ever, calling and saying, I am the way, the truth, and the life.' And here, Florry, is another extract from the same book still more conclusive—' Whom shall I look to as my mediator? Shall I go to angels? Many have tried this, and have been fond of visions, and have deserved to be the sport of the illusions which they loved. The true mediator, whom in thy secret mercy thou hast shown to the humble, and hast sent, that by his example they might also learn humility, the man Christ Jesus, hath appeared a mediator between mortal sinners and the immortal Holy One, that he might justify the ungodly, and deliver them from death.' Yet in your manuals you are directed to say, 'Mother of God, command thy son;' and one of your prayers, Florry, is as follows: 'Hail, Holy Queen! Mother of Mercy—our life, our sweetness, and our hope! To thee do we cry, poor banished sons of Eve, to thee do we send up our sighs, mourning and weeping in the valley of tears. Turn thee, most gracious Advocate, thy eyes of mercy toward us.' And at vespers you say,

'Hail, Mary! queen of heavenly spheres,
Hail! whom the angelic host reveres!'

Florry, in all candor, let us investigate this subject; we will consult both the Bible and the Fathers, or, if you prefer it, by the words of the latter only we will decide; for truth we are searching."

"Mary, let me read a second time those passages from St. Augustine. Strange I should have been so deceived," she continued, as having perused them, she returned the book to her cousin.

"Florry, can you perceive any encouragement there given to the practice of invocation? Does not St. Augustine expressly denounce it?"

"There can be no doubt of his sentiments on this point; but Mary, this is only one decision, when I have been assured that the united voices of many Fathers established it without a doubt, even supposing there was no authority in Holy writ for such a custom—which, however, we have, for did not Jacob wrestle with an angel, and did not his blessing desend upon him?"

"But Christ had not then died; neither had the Christian dispensation succeeded to the old Jewish rites and customs. If you will turn to Jeremiah, you will also read how the curse of God was pronounced against the idolators who offered incense to the Queen of Heaven: yet you do the same. Still, by the tradition of the elders, we will judge. Hear the words of Paulinus on this subject—' Paul is not a mediator; he is an embassador for Christ. John intercedes not, but declares that this mediator is the propitiation for our sin. The Son of Almighty God, because he redeemed us with the price of his blood, is justly called the true Redeemer.' Again the great and good Ambrose—' We follow thee, Lord Jesus, but draw us up that we may follow. No one rises without thee. Let us seek him, and embrace his feet, and worship him, that he may say to us, Fear not. I am the remission of sin. I am the light, I am the life. He that cometh to me shall not see death; because he is the fullness of divinity.' One more, Florry—' Come to yourselves again, ye wretched transgressors! Return ye blind to your light!' Shall we not believe God, when he swears that neither Noah, nor Daniel, nor Job, shall deliver one son or daughter by their righteousness. For this end he makes the declaration, that none might put confidence in the intercession of saints. Ye fools! who run to Rome to seek there for the intercession of an Apostle. When will ye be wise ? What would St. Augustine say of you, whom ye have so often quoted ? Such, Florry, are the words of the celebrated Claud of Turin; but as he is regarded by your church somewhat as a reformer, I will just read one passage from Anselm, whose orthodoxy no Papist ever questioned. Speaking of the intercession of Christ—' If the people sin a thousand times, they need no other Saviour; because this suffices for all things, and cleanses from all sin.' Florry, we have jointly admired the character of one of the earliest martyrs, St. Cyprian. Will you hear him on this subject ?—' Christ, if it be possible, let us all follow. Let us be baptized in his name. He opens to us the way of life. He bring us back to Paradise. He leads us to the heavenly kingdom. Redeemed by his blood, we shall be the blessed of God the Father.' Yet you say in your prayers, ' We fly to thy patronage, oh! holy Mother of God!' And again——

'Hail, sacred gate.'

Florence, you have cited the Fathers: by their own words are you not convinced as to intercession?"

" Mary, I was asking myself if vital Christianity could exist in any church which allows such a system of deceit on the part of its clergy? for deceived I assuredly have been."

" You should remember, Florry, that the promulgation of Papal doctrines, and the aggrandizement of the Romish church, is the only aim of its priesthood; consequently, all means which conduce to this great object are unscrupulously employed. Even crime is sanctioned where the good of the church can be promoted."

" Surely, Mary, you can not mean what you say? Crime sanctioned by the Romish clergy! Impossible! How dare you make such an assertion?"

" It doubtless strikes you, Florry, as strangely uncharitable and unchristian; yet, if you will consult the records of the past, I venture to say you will think very differently. What memorable event occurred on one of your saints' days—the 24th of August, 1572? At dead of night the signal was given, and the Papal ministers of France perpetrated the foulest deed that stains the page of history. Thirty thousand Huguenots were butchered in their beds. And what distinguished the murderer from the doomed victim? A white cross on the hat of the former. How did Imperial Rome receive the tidings of this massacre? The cannons were discharged, the Pope ordered a jubilee and grand procession, and caused a *Te Deum* to be chanted. I ask you Florry, was not this sanctioning crime? Again, how died the great Henry IV? The celebrated edict of Nantes sealed his doom, and the infamous Ravaillac, for the good of the Romish church, conveniently forgot the commandment of Jehovah, and meritoriously assassinated him. Florry, I have myself heard a Papist say, 'that whatever her priest commanded, she would unhesitatingly perform.' Shocked at the broad assertion, I replied: 'You surely do not know what you are saying. Obey the priest in all things! Why, you would not commit murder at his command?' 'Certainly I would, if my priest bid me; for if I obey him, I can not do wrong.' I know this to be true; and I ask you what is the inference? You admit that you have been deceived. Pious frauds were committed in the time of Ambrose and Chrysostom; yet hear what St. Augustine says: 'Lying is the saying of one thing, and thinking of another;' and in all cases, even for most pious purposes, he excludes lying as unchristian and anti-scriptural."

Florence was leaning with clasped hands on the table, gazing intently at her cousin; while Mary knelt on the other side, her hand resting on the large family Bible. The light fell full on her pale face as she knelt; her chestnut curls half vailing the pure white cheek, and the dark-blue eyes, earnest, and yet almost angelic, in their gentle, loving expression.

"Oh, Florry! need I implore you in future to look to Christ alone as the author of our salvation?"

"One more question, Mary. Is there not a passage in Revelations substantiating the doctrine of intercession? Father Mazzolin assured me the testimony was conclusive in favor of that practice."

"The passages to which you allude are these: 'And another angel came and stood at the altar, having a golden censor; and there was given unto him much incense, that he should offer it, with the prayers of all saints, upon the golden altar which was before the throne. And the smoke of the incense which came with the prayers of the saints ascended up before God out of the angel's hand.' No word of intercession occurs here; and are we not as free to suppose that the prayers so offered were in their own behalf as that of their friends? Had it been as the Padre tells you, would not St. John have said intercession or prayers in behalf of others?"

"Mary, can you have mistaken the passage? This cannot be his boasted testimony."

"I know that these two verses are highly prized by Papists, as establishing the doctrine in question; yet I cannot see them in that light—can you?"

"No, no; and if these are the strongest arguments they can adduce in the defense of invocation, I reject it as a remnant of the dark ages, during which period it certainly crept into the church."

" If you do this, Florry, you cause the whole fabric to totter, for on this doctrine, as a foundation, rests the arch, of which confession is the keystone."

"' Confess ye your sins, one to another,' is very strong in our favor, Mary ?"

" Florry, we are searching for truth, and let us in all humility and candor investigate this particularly important point. It seems to me that St. James's meaning is this—when we have offended or harmed our fellow-men or brethren, we should make all the amends in our power; confess our faults unto them; implore their pardon, and abstain from offensive conduct in future. Do you not think that if he intended us to interpret it differently, he would have said—' Confess your faults unto your priest, and he will give you absolution.' Setting aside all bias, do you not think this reasonable; the more so, when we call to mind those words of our Saviour in his sermon on the mount: ' Therefore, if thou bring thy gift to the altar, and there rememberest that thy brother hath aught against thee, leave there thy gift before the altar, and go thy way; first be reconciled to thy brother, and then come and offer thy gift.' If our Lord had intended the ordinance of confession, would he not have said on this occasion, ' First confess thy sins unto thy priest, and when he has absolved thee, then come with clean hands and offer thy gift.' Mark the difference, and ask your own heart if there is any encouragement here for confessing to your Padre?"

"If this passage of James were all we could adduce in favor of confession, I should think with you, Mary; yet it is not so. When about to dismiss his Apostles on their errands of mercy, Christ said to them—'Peace be with you; as my Father hath sent me, even so I send you:' and when he had breathed upon them, he said unto them—'Receive ye the Holy Ghost; whosesoever sins ye remit, they are remitted unto them, and whosesoever sins ye retain, they are retained.' Now Mary, do you not plainly perceive that the power of forgiving sin was conferred upon the Apostles?"

"Most assuredly I do; and avow my belief that they were enabled to forgive sin, and at the same time other miraculous powers were conferred on the 'Twelve.' 'Then he called his twelve disciples together, and gave them power and authority over all devils, and to cure diseases.' We know that they cast out devils, restored the blind, and raised the dead. Power to forgive sin was one among many wonderful gifts conferred upon them. Yet you do not believe that the power of raising the dead was transmitted to posterity. How, then, can you say the gift of absolution was?"

"But, Mary, Christ says in another place—'Thou art Peter: and upon this rock I will build my church, and the gates of Hell shall not prevail against it. And I will give unto thee the keys of the kingdom of heaven, and whatsoever thou shalt bind on earth shall be bound in heaven, and whatsoever thou shalt loose on earth shall be loosed in heaven.'"

"I perfectly agree with you, Florry, in believing that St. Peter had miraculous powers bestowed on him by our Saviour; but it seems absurd to suppose that those powers were perpetuated in the ministers of the Roman Catholic Church. Our Saviour said, what 'Peter loosed, should be loosed in heaven,' and not what Peter's successors loosed should be observed and loosed in heaven. We should not judge of Christ's views by isolated passages, but rather from all his teachings; for if we did, what would you say to the verse just below those already quoted, 'And he said unto Peter, get thee behind me Satan, thou art an offense unto me, for thou savorest not the things which be of God, but those that be of men.' But this is wandering from the subject. In St. Augustine's Confessions, though I admit somewhat abridged, I find nothing relating to confessing to priests. This passage alone appears: 'O Lord, thou knowest!—have I not confessed my sins to thee? and hast thou not pardoned the iniquity of my heart?' Speaking of a sudden illness during his boyhood, he says he eagerly desired baptism, fearing to die, and his mother was about to comply with his request, when he quickly recovered. Now had he considered confession necessary, would he not have urged it upon all who read his Confessions, which you will mark, Florry, were not made to a priest, but obviously to God himself."

There followed a long pause, while Florence dropt her face in her hands, and sighed heavily.

"Florry, it is very late; our candle has burnt low—see, it is flickering in the socket; we have not heeded the lapse of time." She rose and replaced the books she had been consulting.

"Mary, Mary! why have you shaken my faith? I had thought to find comfort in future, but you have torn my hope from me, and peace flies with the foundations which you have removed!"

"Florry, you have been blinded, deceived. They have cried unto you, Peace! peace! when there was no peace. But oh! there is a source of rest and strength, and comfort, which is to be attained not by confession, or the intercession of the dead or living, but by repentance for the past, and an active, trusting faith in the meditation of our blessed Lord Jesus Christ."

CHAPTER XVII.

> "The purple clouds
> Are putting on their gold and violet,
> To look the meeter for the sun's bright coming.
> How hallowed is the hour of morning! Meet—
> Ay! beautifully meet—for the pure prayer."
>
> *Willis.*

Morn broke in the East; or, in the beautiful language of the Son of Fingal, "Sol's yellow hair streamed on the Eastern gale." Awakened by the first chirping of the feathered tribe, Florence rose as the gray morning light stole into her chamber, and seating herself at the window, looked out on the town before her. Quiet reigned as yet, broken only by the murmuring and gurgling of the river, which rolled swiftly on, just below their little gate. How delightful to her seemed

> "The cool, the fragrant, and the silent hour
> To meditation due."

Calmly she now weighed the conversation of the preceding night, and engrossed in earnest thought, sat gazing out till the Orient shone resplendent, and an October sun poured his rays gloriously around her. Then she knelt, and prayed as she had never done before. She sought the " pure fountain of light," and implored strength and guidance in her search after truth. Rising, her glance fell on her sleeping cousin, and she was struck with the change which within the last month had taken place in her appearance. Approaching the bed, she lifted the masses of chestnut hair that clung to the damp brow. As she looked on the pure, pale face, there came a gush of tenderness into her soul, and bending, she imprinted a long, warm kiss. Mary stirred, and opened her eyes.

"Ah, Florry, you are up earlier than usual." She closed them again, murmuring slowly, "I feel as though I had no strength remaining; I can scarcely lift my head."

"Sleep, Mary, if you can. I will shut out the light, and call you again after a wh'le."

"No, Florry, I must not give way to such feelings; indeed they are getting quite too common of late; I can't think what makes me so weak and feverish."

An hour later, as they stood together at the door of their little dining-room, a body of Mexican cavalry dashed furiously past their gate. The cousins looked full at each other. Then Florence said in a low, calm tone: "You are right, Mary; we will go from this place; I feel now that it is for the best." She averted her face; but Mary saw an expression of keen agony resting there. "Florry, let us consult Mrs. Carlton. She will advise us what would be best to do in this emergency."

"Go and see her yourself; I can not. Whatever you decide upon I will agree to. Oh! Mary, how desolate and unprotected we are."

"No, not while there is an Almighty One to watch over us. But, Florry, I am much troubled about Aunt Lizzy. I mentioned our wish to leave here, and she opposed it strenuously, on the grounds that the Padre had promised his protection. Now what are we to do?"

"Go to Mrs. Carlton's, Mary, and I will convince aunt that it is best we should remove from here immediately. You need apprehend no difficulty on her part. As you return from Mrs. Carlton's, meet me in the church-yard."

"Florry, do not go till I come home; or, if you prefer it, let us go there at once."

" No, Mary, I wish to be there alone."

" But I am afraid it is not quite safe for you to venture out so far from home."

" I fear nothing: who would harm a daughter beside her father's grave ?"

Mary sighed heavily, but offered no further opposition. Her walk to Mrs. Carlton's was a sad one, for her heart clung to the scenes she had learned to love so well, and the prospect of departure, and the uncertainty of the future, weighed heavily on her heart, and made her step unwontedly slow. She found her friend alone, and much depressed. Mrs. Carlton clasped her tenderly in her arms, while the tears rolled silently down her cheeks.

" I hope nothing has happened to distress you ?" said Mary, anxiously.

" You are the very one I wished to see. Mr. Carlton said, this morning, that he was unwilling for me to remain here any longer, as our troops are marching to attack the Alamo. He says he will take us to Washington, and I could not bear the idea of leaving you here."

" I have come to consult you on this subject; for some of my Mexican friends have advised us to leave San Antonio; and not knowing where or how to go, concluded to come and see you. But Washington is far, very far from here. How will we ever reach it in these unsettled times ?"

" Mr. Carlton and Frank have gone to make all necessary preparation for our immediate departure. We will have two tents, and carry such cooking utensils and provisions as are needful for a tedious journey: one wagon is all we hope to obtain for conveying these. I suppose we shall all ride horseback; for you know there is not a carriage in the town. Frank does not wish us to leave this place, for he suggested your coming to remain with us till these stormy times were over. But this is not a suitable home for you. Surely your cousin and aunt will consent to accompany us?"

"Yes, I think so; for Florry left it entirely with me, and certainly we should go now."

"I am very glad to hear you say so, Mary; not only upon your own account, but also for Frank. He will consider himself bound to accompany you; for he promised your dying uncle to watch over you both with a brother's care, and otherwise he could not be induced to leave San Antonio at this crisis. He seems completely rapt in the issue of the contest; and would you believe it, Mary, he is anxious to enlist; but my entreaties have as yet prevented him."

"Dear Mrs. Carlton, there is no obligation resting on him to go with us. He has been very kind and careful, and though deeply grateful, we could not consent to his leaving against his own inclinations. Oh, no! we could not allow this. Yet should he remain, what may be the result? Oh! Mrs. Carlton, this is terrible."

Mary's cheek was very pale, and her lips quivered convulsively, while the small hands clasped each other tightly.

"Mary, for my sake, use your influence with him in favor of going to Washington. I can't go in peace, and feel that he is here exposed to such imminent danger, for when I am gone, what will restrain him? Mary, Mary! do not deter him, if he feels it incumbent on him to see you to a place of safety."

"Mrs. Carlton, you can appreciate the peculiar position in which I am placed. Florry and I would shrink from drawing him away, in opposition to his wishes, particularly when there is no danger attendant on our traveling; for with you and Mr. Carlton we would feel no apprehension; and even if we did, we could not consent to such a sacrifice on his part. Yet I sympathize with you, most sincerely, and will willingly do all that in propriety I can to alleviate your sorrow; but knowing his sentiments, how could I advise, or even acquiesce in his going?"

"My pure-hearted girl, forgive a request made so thoughtlessly. I had not considered, as I should have done; yet you can appreciate the anxious feelings which dictated it." As she spoke, Mrs. Carlton clasped her friend to her heart, and wept on her shoulder. No tear dimmed Mary's eye; yet that she suffered, none who looked on her pale brow and writhing lips could doubt. As she raised her head to reply, Dr. Bryant entered, and started visibly on seeing her. Mrs. Carlton endeavored to regain her composure: and with a slightly faltering voice, asked how he succeeded in procuring horses?

"Better than I had hoped," was the rejoinder; and

he held out his hand to Mary. She gave him hers, now cold as ice. He held it a moment and pressed it gently, saying: " You see my sister is going to run away on the first intimation of danger. I hope she has not infected you with her fears; though to judge from your looks I should almost predict a stampede in another direction."

" Indeed, you are quite right. Florry and I are going with her; though we had decided on leaving before we knew she intended doing so."

" Ah! you did not seem to apprehend any immediate danger when we conversed on this subject a few days since. What has changed your views ?"

" I have been warned not to risk the dangers attendant on the approaching conflict by a Mexican friend whose attachment I have every reason to believe i. sincere; and besides, it needed but little to augment my fears; and Florry and I concluded, if practicable, to remove to a place of greater safety."

" Can you be ready within two days, think you, Miss Mary ? for, if we leave at all, it is advisable that we do so immediately."

" Oh, yes! I know that we can be ready by that time."

" Let me see—how many additional horses shall we need ? Yourself, your cousin, and aunt, and myself."

Mary looked eagerly at Mrs. Carlton; but she had averted her head; and for a moment a terrible struggle within kept the gentle girl silent.

" Dr. Bryant, I know you do not wish to leave here

at this juncture, intensely interested as you are in the event, and I fear you are sacrificing your own wishes for our benefit. Let me beg you to consult your inclinations, and do not feel it in the least incumbent on you to attend us, particularly when we are in the kind care of Mr. Carlton; and you have already done so much toward contributing to our comfort."

"Thank you for your consideration. Nevertheless, I shall not rest satisfied till I place you in safety on the banks of the Brazos. One of my greatest pleasures has been to render you service, and you would not abridge them, I hope, by refusing my company on your journey?"

Mary's eyes were fixed earnestly on his face while he spoke, and though there was no change in his kind, gentle tone, there came an undefinable expression over his noble countenance—an expression in which coldness and sorrow predominated. She could not understand him; yet a shudder crept through her frame and a sensation of acute pain stole into her heart. She felt as though a barrier had suddenly risen between them, yet could not analyze the cause.

"Your servants will take all possible care of the house and furniture during your absence, which, I hope, will be but temporary. They will not be molested; and I am afraid we could not conveniently carry two additional persons. What think you of this arrangement?"

"I think with you, that under existing circumstances the servants could not well accompany us;

and though they will incur no danger, I regret the necessity of leaving them, particularly should they object "

" I hope you will find no difficulty in arranging everything to your entire satisfaction previous to our departure. You and my sister must consult as to all minor points, and I must look to our preparations. My respects to your cousin. I will see you again to-morrow;" and bidding her good morning, he turned away.

" Oh, such a weight is lifted from my heart!" exclaimed Mrs. Carlton. " I can now exert myself as I am called on to do."

" Florry will be waiting for me, and we have much to do at home; so good-by," and Mary lifted her pale face for a farewell kiss.

Mrs. Carlton affectionately embraced her, and bidding her " make all speed," they parted

---

CHAPTER XVIII.

" There is a soul just delivered from purgatory! It was found to be a frog dressed in red flannel."—*Kirwan.*

FLORENCE having succeeded, as she imagined, in convincing her aunt that it was advisable to remove from San Antonio, slowly proceeded to the churchyard, little dreaming that the door had scarce closed behind her, ere Aunt Lizzy, with swift steps, directed her way to the house of the Padre. He was writing, but gave his attention, and heard, with ill-disguised chagrin, that Florence distrusted his promised protection.

"Does she doubt in matters of faith, think you?" he eagerly inquired.

"Indeed, Padre, I can not say. All I know is, that she and Mary sat till midnight, reading and talking, and she has not seemed like herself since."

"Where shall I find Florence?" said he, taking his hat.

"In the church-yard, I think, beside her father's grave."

"Say nothing to her, but apparently acquiesce in her plans; and, above all, do not let her dream that you have told me these things."

Ah, Florence! who may presume to analyze the anguish of your tortured heart, as you throw yourself in such abandonment of grief on the tomb of your lost parent? The luxuriant grass, swaying to and fro in the chill October blast, well-nigh concealed the bent and drooping form as she knelt and laid her head on the cold granite.

"My father! oh, my father!" and tears, which she had not shed before, fell fast, and somewhat eased the desolate, aching heart. Florence had not wept before in many years; and now that the fountain was unsealed, she strove not to repress the tears which seemed to lift and bear away the heavy weight which had so long crushed her spirits.

What a blessing it is to be able to weep; and happy are they who can readily give vent to tears, and thus exhaust their grief! Such can never realize the intensity of anguish which other natures suffer —natures to whom this great relief is denied, and who must keep the withering, scorching agony pent up within the secret chambers of their desolate, aching hearts. Sobs and tears are not for these. No, no; alone and in darkness they must wrestle with their grief, crush it down into their inmost soul, and with a calm exterior go forth to meet the world. But ah! the flitting, wintry smile, the short, constrained laugh, the pale brow marked with lines of mental anguish, will ofttimes tell of the smouldering ruin. . . .

"My daughter, God has appointed me in place of the parent he has taken hence; turn to me, and our most holy church, and you will find comfort such as naught else can afford."

Florence sprang to her feet, and shuddered at the sound of his low, soft voice. The Padre marked the shudder, and the uneasy look which accompanied it: "Padre, I have confessed, and I have prayed to almost every saint in the Calendar, and I have had your prayers in addition to my own; yet I find no comfort. No joy has stolen to my heart as you promised it inevitably would."

"My daughter, if peace has not descended on thy spirit, I fear you have not been devout. Tell me truly, if you have not doubted in matters of faith, for our most holy Mother ever grants the prayers of her faithful and loving children?"

"I have searched the Bible, and I nowhere find authority for invoking saints or the Virgin."

"I can convince you, without doubt, that there is such authority—nay, command."

"'Tis useless, you may save yourself the trouble; for my mind is clearly made up that we have not even the sanction of the Fathers."

"Holy Mary, pardon her unbelief, and send down light into her darkened soul!"

Florence fixed her eyes full upon him, and replied —" Christ expressly declares 'I am the light, I am the life.'"

"Daughter, your heretic cousin has done you a great injury. May God protect you, and forgive her blasphemy."

"She needs no forgiveness, for she is pure in heart before God and truthful in all things."

The swarthy cheek of the Italian flushed—"Florence, you and your aunt must come and stay at my house till it is safe here; and I doubt not, when you are at leisure to hear me, you will duly repent your hasty speeches. I shall pray God and our Lady to give you a more trusting, believing heart, and intercede with the blessed saints for your entire conversion."

"Not so, Father Mazzolin; we shall leave this place in a very few days, and I have come to bid adieu to the grave of my father; leave me, for I wish to be alone and in peace."

"Do you doubt my will or ability to protect you, my daughter? Beneath my roof no danger can assail."

"We have fully decided to go from here, and further reasoning or entreaty would be vain; accept, however, my thanks for your proffered kindness."

"Girl, you have gone too far! Hear me while I am placable, for I tell you now, without my consent you can not—shall not leave here."

"You have neither right nor power to detain me."

"Have I not? I swear, if you do not hear and abide by what I say, your father's soul will remain forever in purgatory where it justly belongs."

"How dare you make so miserable a threat?" said the calm, clear voice of Mary, who had approached unobserved.

"Cursed believer in a cursed creed, what do you here. Begone, or dread the vengeance I shall surely inflict on so blasphemous and damnable a heretic!"

Winding her arm tightly about Florence's waist, she replied—"'Vengeance is mine, saith the Lord. I will repay;' and though I have never injured you, Padre—even if I had it ill becomes a consecrated priest to utter such language, or so madly to give vent to passion."

"Silence!" thundered the Padre, livid with rage; "I will compass heaven and earth rather than you shall escape me."

"Come, Florry, this is no place for us now; even the church-yard is not sacred. Come home."

"Florence, dare you curse your own father?" The

girl's lips quivered but no sound came forth—she seemed stunned.

"You would usurp the prerogatives of Jehovah, Father Mazzolin; but your threat is vain. You can not bless or damn my uncle at will. How dare you, guilty as you are, hold such impious language?"

For a moment he quailed before the calm, unflinching girl, then seizing Florence's arm, hoarsely exclaimed: "One more chance I give you. Florence, I am your brother—your father, my father. On his death-bed he confessed his sins and discovered his son."

A deep groan burst from Florence's lips, and her slender frame quivered like a reed in a wintry blast. The Padre laid his head on the granite slab which covered the remains of Mr. Hamilton, and continued: "I call God in heaven and all the saints to witness the truth of what I say, and if I prove it not may I sink into perdition. When your father was yet young he made the tour of Europe. Traveling in Italy, he met at Florence a poor but beautiful girl; and she, struck, in turn, by the handsome face of the stranger, left her humble home and listened to the voice of seduction. He remained five months at Florence, and then suddenly left Italy for his native country without apprising the unfortunate woman of his intentions. Hatred succeeded to love, and she vowed vengeance. That woman was my mother; and when ten years had passed, she told me my parentage, and made me swear on the altar of her patron saint that I would fulfill her vow of vengeance. She died and I became a priest of Rome, and in time was sent by my order to Mexico, and thence here to assist my aged and infirm predecessor. I had in my possession a miniature of my father, and no sooner had I met him here than I recognized the base being who had deserted my mother. I kept my peace; but ere he died he confessed that one sin—heavier than everything beside—weighed on his conscience. In the agony and remorse of that hour my mother was revenged. I told my parentage, and he discovered his child. Feeling that I was your brother, he bade you remain here, claim my protection, and follow my advice. But, Florence, hear me—your misery touched my heart; a kindred feeling for you made me desire to serve you; but I swear now that if you hear not my voice, and return to the bosom of our church, your father's soul shall linger in damnation, and my vengeance shall follow you. You know not my power, and woe to you if you defy me!"

Had the spectre-form of the deceased, leaving the shadowy band of the spirit-world, risen on the granite slab before them, the two girls could not have been more startled. Tightly they clung one to another, their eyes riveted on the face of the Padre. There was a long pause; then Florence lifted herself proudly up, and cold and haughty was her tone. "It is not for me to deny your statement. If my father sinned, peace to his memory, and may God forgive him. One so sinful and malignant as yourself can not be invested with divine prerogatives

I have known your intentions with regard to myself since the hour I knelt in confession. I was destined for a convent, and I tacitly acquiesced in your plans, hoping that so secluded from the world I should be comparatively happy; but my feelings are changed on many points, and any further interference from you will be received with the scorn it merits. No love for me actuates your movements, else you would have spared me the suffering of this hour."

" You defy me, then ?"

Florence had turned away, and heeded not his question; but Mary, clasping her hands, looked appealingly in his face: " Oh, Padre, by the tie which you declare exists between yourself and Florry—for the sake of your lost parent—do not put your threat in execution. Spare an unprotected orphan. You will not harm your sister!"

" Know you not, girl, that when a Jesuit priest takes the oath of his order, he tears his heart from his breast and lays it at the feet of his superior? Appeal not to ties of relationship: we repudiate them, and pity is unknown among us."

With a shudder Mary joined her cousin, and rapidly and in perfect silence they retraced their steps homeward. When they reached their gate, Mary would have opened it, but her cousin, taking her hand, led the way to their old seat beside the river.

Florence seated herself as near the water as possible, and then tightly clasping the hand she held, asked in a voice of suppressed emotion: " Tell me, Mary, is there a purgatory ?"

"No, Florry; I think there is less foundation for that doctrine than any advanced by your church."

"Mary, you speak truth, and all that you say I can implicitly believe. Tell me what grounds support the theory?"

"You remember the words of our Saviour, 'All sin shall be forgiven, save blasphemy of the Holy Ghost; that shall not be forgiven, either in this world or the next.' Now Papists argue in this way: Then other sins can be forgiven in another world; there is no sin in heaven, in hell no forgiveness, consequently, there must exist a middle place, or, in other words, a purgatory. Florry, you smile, yet I assure you I have seen this advanced as unanswerable. In the book of Maccabees is a very remarkable passage authorizing prayers for the dead, and on this passage they build their theory and sanction their practice. Yet you know full well it is one of the Apocryphal books rejected by the Jews, because not originally written in their language. It was never quoted by our Saviour, nor even received as inspired by your own church till the Council of Trent, when it was admitted to substantiate the doctrine of purgatory, and sanction prayers for the dead. I admit that on this point St. Augustine's practice was in favor of it; though it was only near the close of his long life that he speaks of the soul of his mother. Yet already history informs us that the practice of praying for the dead was gaining ground in the church, along with image worship. St. Cyprian, who lived long before him, and during a purer state of the church, leaves no doubt on our minds as to his sentiments on that subject; his words are these: 'When ye depart hence, there will be no room for repentance—no method of being reconciled to God. Here eternal life is either lost or won. Here, by the worship of God, and the fruit of faith, provision is made for eternal salvation. And let no man be retarded, either by his sins or years, from coming to obtain it. No repentance is too late while a man remains in this world.' Our Saviour nowhere gives any encouragement of such a doctrine. On the contrary, he said to the dying thief: 'This day shalt thou be with me in Paradise.' I know of no other argument which Papists advance in favor of their darling theory, save the practice of the latter Fathers of their church."

"Mary, I can not believe this doctrine, without further proof of Divine sanction."

"Indeed, Florry, I know of no other reason in its favor, and have long supposed it a system of extortion in connection with indulgences, now used only as a means of gain by the dissolute clergy of the Romish faith. I need scarcely say, that the abuse of this latter doctrine drove Luther to reformation. It is a well-known fact, that in the 16th century, Tetzel, a Dominican monk high in his order, drove through Germany in a wagon, containing two boxes, one holding indulgences, the other the money received for them. You will smile, Florry, when I repeat a translation of the German lines written on the outside of the letter-box:

"'When in this chest the money rings,
The soul straight up to heaven springs.'

Yet the boldness and audacity of his general language was quite in accordance. 'Indulgences,' said he, 'are the most precious of God's gifts. I would not exchange my privileges for those of St. Peter in heaven; for I have saved more souls with my indulgences than he with all his sermons. There is no sin so great that the indulgence will not remit it. Even repentance is not necessary. Indulgences save the dead; for the very moment the money chinks against the bottom of this chest, the soul escapes from purgrtory, and flies to heaven.'

"Yet this inquisitor was high in favor with Pope Leo X. You will say, Florry, that the abuse of a doctrine should be no test of its soundness; and I admit that had he received the punishment he so richly merited it would not; yet this is only one instance among many. We have conversed on the doctrines of the Romish faith merely as theories, should we not now look at the practice? We need not go very far. When Aunt Fanny expressed surprise on seeing our Mexican shepherd eat meat last Friday, did he not reply in extenuation, ' I have paid the priest and can eat meat ?' Now if it was necessary tor him to abstain previously, conld the small sum paid to the Padre exempt him from the duty? Again we see the working of the system: was not Herrara scrupulously exact on the same point ? yet he rose from the table and told a most positive lie. With regard to indulgences, there is not a Papist who will admit that they are a license to sin ? The voice of history declares that 'a regular scale for absolution was graded,' and the fact is authenticated by a recent traveler, who asserts that in the chancel of Santa Croce, at Rome, is hung a catalogue of the indulgences granted to all who worship in that church. Yet your priests will tell you they are the remission of sins already committed. Did not Herrara say, ' I have paid the Padre and can eat meat ?' Now I ask you if this is not a license to commit what would otherwise be considered a heinous offense by all devout Papists ?"

" Relying implicitly on what the Padre asserted, Mary, I have never investigated these subjects as I should have done, before giving my credence and support; but of the doctrine in question I can henceforth entertain but one opinion—a detestable and famous method of filling the papal coffers; for since you have led me to think on this subject, I clearly remember that a large portion of the enormous expense incurred by the building, ornamenting, and repairing of St. Peter's, was defrayed by money obtained through the sale of indulgences. Oh, Mary, how could I have been so deluded—allowed myself to be so deceived!" She took from her pocket the rosary and crucifix which had been given to her father, and threw them impatiently into the river gurgling at her feet.

" The perfect harmony with which the entire system works is unparalleled in the civil, religious, or political annals of the world. A complete espionage is exercised in papal countries, from the Adriatic to the Californian gulf. And the greater portion of this is accomplished by means of the confessional. The Superior at Rome can become, at pleasure, as perfectly conversant with your domestic arrangements, and the thousand incidents which daily occur, as you or I, who are cognizant of them. To what is all this tending? Ah, Florry, look at the blood-stained records of the past. The voices of slaughtered thousands, borne to us across the waste of centuries, bid us remember the Duke of Alva, the Albigensian crusade, the massacre of St. Bartholemew, and the blazes of Smithfield. Ignatius Loyola! happy would it have been for millions lost, and millions yet to be, hadst thou perished at the siege of Pampeluna. Florry, contrast Italy and Germany, Spain and Scotland, and look at Portugal, and South America and Mexico, and oh, look at this benighted town! A fairer spot by nature the face of earth cannot boast; yet mark the sloth, the penury, the degradation of its people, the misery that prevails. And why? Because they languish under the iron rule of the papal see—iron, because it admits of no modification. Entire supremacy over both body and soul, or total annihilation of their power. May the time speedily come when they shall spurn their oppressors, and trample their yoke in the dust, as their transatlantic brethren will ultimately do. Oh, Florry, does not your heart yearn toward benighted Italy? Italy, once so beautiful and noble—once the acknowledged mistress of the world, as she sat in royal magnificence, enthroned on her seven hills; now a miserable waste, divided between petty sovereigns, and a by-word for guilt and degradation! The glorious image lies a ruin at our feet! for the spirit that gave beauty and strength, and shed a halo of splendor round its immortal name, has fled afar, perhaps forever; banished by the perfidious system of Papacy—that sworn foe to liberty, ecclesiastical or political.

"How incomprehensible the apathy with which the English regard the promulgation of Puseyism in their church! It is stealing silently but swiftly to the very heart of their ecclesiastical institutions, and total subversion will ultimately ensue. That Americans should contemplate without apprehension the gradual increase of papal power is not so astonishing, for this happy land has never groaned beneath its iron sway. But that the descendants of Latimer and of Ridley, of Hooper and of Cranmer, should tamely view the encroachments of this monster hydra, is strange indeed. Do not imagine, Florry, that I doubt the sincerity of all who belong to the Chutch of Rome. I know and believe that there are many earnest and conscientious members—of this there cannot be a doubt; yet it is equally true, that the most devoted Papists are to be found among the most ignorant, bigoted, and superstitious of men. The masses of your church are deceived with pretended miracles and wondrous legends, such as the one currently reported respecting the holy house of Loretto, which seems so migratory, and flies hundreds of miles in a night. These marvelous tales are credited by the uneducated; yet no enlightened man or woman of the present age, who has fully investigated this subject, can say with truth that they conscientiously believe the doctrines of the Romish Church to be those taught by our Saviour, or its practices in accordance with the general tenor of the Bible. This may seem a broad assertion, yet none who calmly consider the subject in all its bearings, and consult the page of history, will pronounce it a hasty one."

" Yet remember, Mary, that the sect in question is proverbial for charitable institutions. One vital principle is preserved. Surely this is a redeeming virtue. Catholics are untiring in schemes of benevolence and philanthrophy."

" You will start, and perhaps condemn me, when I reply that their boasted charity is but the mask behind which they disseminate the doctrines of the Romish Church. I may appear very uncharitable in the expression of this opinion; yet hear me, Florry; facts are incontrovertible. If you will think a moment, you can not fail to remember Patrick, the porter at our friend Mrs. D——'s. Having received a dangerous wound in his foot, he was sent to the hospital, where several of the nurses were Sisters of Charity. He remained nearly a month, and on his return related to Mrs. D——, in my presence, some of the circumstances of his long illness. His words made a lasting impression on my mind:

" ' Indeed, and I am glad enough to come home,

ma'am; for never was I treated worse in my life. The first week, Sister Agnes, who nursed in my room, was kind and tender as could be, and thought, I, if ever angels come to earth, this good woman is one; but I can tell ye I did not think so long: she read some saints' lives to us, and asked me if I was a Catholic. I said no, I was no Catholic. Then she tried every way to make me one, and told me if I refused I would surely die and go to purgatory. Faith! the more she talked that way, the more I wouldn't be a Catholic; and then she just let me alone, and not another thing would she do for me. I might call from then till now, and never a step would she come, or nurse me a bit. It is no good care of hers that has brought me back alive and well: I tell you, Sister Agnes won't do for any but Catholics.'

"Florry, is such charity akin to that taught by the Bible? Catholics boast of their asylums; and by means of fairs and suppers, large amounts are annually collected for the support of these numerous institutions. I have been told by a directress of a Protestant orphan asylum, that on one occasion a squalid woman, accompanied by two boys, presented herself and entreated that her children might be received into the asylum. The unhappy mother informed the directress that she was a Roman Catholic, and had claimed the protection of her own sect; 'but,' said she, tearfully, 'Indeed I had no money to pay for their entrance, and they refused to take my children.'

"Such, Florry, is their boasted charity; and I

might add, their lives are little in accordance with the spirit inculcated by our Saviour, who said, 'When ye do your alms, let not your left hand know what your right hand doeth.' There are thousands who daily dispense charities of various kinds; yet they do not term themselves Sisters of Charity; neither promenade the streets in a garb so antiquated and peculiar as to excite attention, or elicit encomiums on their marvelously holy lives and charitable deeds. Do not suppose, Florry, because I speak thus, that I doubt the sincerity of all who enroll themselves as Sisters. I do believe that there are many pious and conscientious women thus engaged; yet they are but tools of the priests, and by them placed in these institutions for the purpose of making proselytes."

A pause ensued, and Florence paced slowly along the bank. Somewhat abruptly she replied:

"Yet you will admit, Mary, that we owe much to the monks, by whose efforts light and knowledge were preserved during the dark ages? But for them every vestige of literature, every record of the past, would inevitably have been lost."

"Tell me, Florry, what caused the dark ages? Was it not the gradual withdrawal of light and knowledge—the crushing, withering influence exerted on the minds of men? And tell me if this influence was not wielded by the priests of Rome—corrupted, fallen Rome? During the dark period in question, papal power was at its height; the thunders of the Vatican were echoed from the Adriatic to the

Atlantic—from the Mediterranean to the North Sea. An interdict of its profligate Pope clothed cities, and kingdoms, and empires in mourning; the churches were closed, the dead unburied, and no rite, save that of baptism, performed. Ignorance and superstition reigned throughout the world; and it is said, that in the ninth century scarce a person was to be found in Rome itself who knew even the alphabet. Yet monasteries crowned every eminence, and dotted the vales of southern Europe. The power of the priesthood was supreme. Florry, I do admit that what remained of light and learning was hid in the cell of the anchorite; not disseminated, but effectually concealed. They forgot our Saviour's injunction—'Let your light shine before men.' Oh! Florry, did not teachers of the dark ages put their light under a bushel? Dark ages will ever follow the increase of papal power. It is part of their system to keep the masses in ignorance. How truly it has been said that Rome asked but one thing, and that Luther denied her—' A fulcrum of ignorance on which to rest that lever by which she can balance the world.' They dare not allow their people light and knowledge; and what to others was indeed a dark age, is regarded by the priests of Rome as a golden season. Can you point to a single papal country which is not enveloped in the black cloud of superstition and crime? To Italy, and Spain, and Portugal, the dark ages have not passed away; neither will they, till liberty of conscience is allowed, and the Bible permitted in the hands of the laity.

Under papal rule, those unfortunate nations will never rise from their degradation; for their masters and teachers 'love darkness rather than light, because their deeds are evil.' It has often been said by those who fail properly to consider this subject, that the Roman Catholic schools and colleges which abound in the United States are far superior to similar Protestant institutions. Why do not these very superior teachers disseminate knowledge at home? Why do they not first enlighten the Spaniards, ere they cross the Atlantic to instruct American pupils? The ignorance of Neapolitans is proverbial; yet Naples is the peculiarly favored city of Romanism. Tell me why these learned professors do not teach their own people? Florry, papal institutions in America are but branches of the Propaganda. They but come to proselyte. I have heard it repeatedly averred of a certain nunnery, 'that no efforts were made to affect the religious views of the pupils.' Yet I know that such is not the case. They are far too politic openly to attack the religion; yet secretly it is undermined. I will tell you how, Florry, for you look wonderingly at me. Prizes are awarded for diligence, and application; and these prizes are books, setting forth in winning language the doctrines of their church. I have seen one of these which was given to M—— K——, and I also read it most carefully. It was entitled 'Alethea; or, a Defense of Catholic Doctrines.' Yet most indignantly they deny any attempts toward proselyting the pupils intrusted to their care."

"Who will deny the truth of your statements, Mary? Yet, if such are the facts, how can the world be so utterly ignorant of, or indifferent to them? Strange that they can thus regard a subject so fraught with interest to every lover of liberty—to every patriot."

"Florry, Papists are unacquainted with these things; for, begirt with darkening, crushing influence, they are effectually secluded from even a wandering ray of light on this subject. The avenue through which all information is conveyed at the present day is barred to them. Books are denied to the Catholic laity. You may ask how this is effected in this enlightened and liberal age. The prelates of Rome, who long ago resorted to ignorance as their bulwark, are ever on the alert. No sooner is a new publication announced, than it is most carefully perused by them; and if calculated to point out the fallacy of their doctrines, or depict their abuse of power, a papal bull is forthwith issued, prohibiting all Catholics from reading the heretical book. The writings of the prince of novelists, Walter Scott, which are universally read by other sects, are peremptorily refused to all Papists. And why? Because many of his darts are aimed at their profligate priesthood. Now if, as they tell their people, these are but slanderous attacks on their religion, surely the shafts would fall harmless on the armor of truth. Why then so strenuously oppose their reading such works! Florry, the trite adage, 'Truth is the hardest of all to bear,' is applicable to these prelates of papacy; who, knowing their danger, are fully resolved to guard the avenues of light and knowledge. The Pope of imperial Rome, surrounded as he is with luxury, magnificence, and hosts of scarlet-liveried cardinals, who stand in readiness to convey his mandates to the remotest corners of the earth, has been made to tremble on his throne by the pen of feeble women. The truthful delineations of Charlotte Elizabeth startled his Holiness of the Vatican and the assistant conclave of learned cardinals trembling lest their laity of the Green Isle should catch a glimpse of light. A bull was quickly fulminated against her heretical productions. Alas! when will the Romish Church burst the iron bands which begirt her?

"The world at large—I mean the world as composed of Protestants, latitudinarians, politicians, statesmen, and fashionable dunces, are in a great measure acquainted with these facts; but knowing the rapidly increasing power of papal Rome, and the vast influence already wielded in this happy land by its priesthood, they prefer to float along with the tide, rather than vigorously resist this blasting system of ignorance, superstition, and crime which, stealthily approaching from the east and from the west, will unite and crush the liberties of our glorious Republic. As patriots, they are called on to oppose strenuously its every encroachment—yet they dare not; for should they venture to declaim against its errors, they endanger their popularity and incur the risk of defeat at an ensuing election. Florry, I was once conversing on this subject with a lady who had recently visited Europe, and inquired of her if she had not marked the evils and abuses which existed in the papal dominions through which she traveled. She whisperingly replied—' Certainly, my dear, I could not fail to mark the ignorance and degradation which prevailed, but I never speak of it, because, you know, it makes one very unpopular.' Here, Florry, you have the key to the mystery. Americans quietly contemplate this momentous subject, and silently view the abuses which are creeping into our communities, because if they expose them, it is at the hazard of becoming unpopular."

"Mary, can I ever, ever forget the hour in the church-yard?" Florence sadly said, as they rose and proceeded to the house. "Oh! it seems branded on my brain; yet I must cast this new grief from me, far enough of anguish was mine before. Still I feel that there is a path just ahead, and it seems lighted up. But a slight barrier intervenes, and when that is passed all will be well. Pray for me, Mary, that I may be enabled to lead the life of a Christian, and last die the death of the righteous."

Clasping tightly the hand which rested in her own, Mary replied:

"While life remains, it shall indeed be my prayer that you may be blessed on earth, and rewarded in heaven. Oh, Florry, I thank God that the scales have fallen from your eyes, and that truth shines brightly before you." She stopped suddenly, and pressed her hand to her side while the pale brow wrinkled with pain.

"I have been talking too much, there is a suffocating sensation here."

"It is only momentary, I hope."

Mary shook her head, and smiled sadly: "I don't know, Florry; I have felt strangely of late."

That evening, as the household were busily preparing for their intended departure, Dr. Bryant abruptly entered, and informed them, with a clouded brow, that removal was impossible, as he could not procure a pair of horses for any price.

"It is perfectly unaccountable what has possessed the Mexican from whom I purchased as many as I thought necessary. We agreed as to price, and they were to be sent this afternoon; but about two hours ago, he came to me, and declared that he had changed his mind, and would not part with them. I offered double the original amount, but he said money was no inducement. I strove to borrow or hire for any given time, but every proposal was peremptorily declined, and as it is impossible to leave here, I came over to entreat you to remain with my sister, at least for a few days, till we can determine what is advisable to do."

His proposal was accepted, and the ensuing day saw them inmates of Mrs. Carlton's.

CHAPTER XIX.

"We're the sons of sires that baffled
Crowned and mitred tyranny:
They defied the field and scaffold
For their birth-rights—so will we!"
—*Campbell.*

THE issue of the engagement of the 8th October placed Goliad, with valuable munitions, in the hands of the Texans. Many and joyous acclamations rose from their camp, hope beamed on every face, and sanguine expectations were entertained of a speedy termination of the conflict. Showly the little band proceeded toward Bexar, receiving daily accessions from head-quarters, and girding themselves for a desperate struggle. General Cos, fully appreciating the importance of the post he held, made active preparation for its defense, never doubting, however, that the strong fortifications of the Alamo would prove impregnable to assailants so feeble numerically. Under the direction of the cautious Spaniard, the town already assumed a beleaguered aspect, and in addition to the watchman stationed on the observatory of the fortress, a sentinel paced to and fro on the flat roof of the gray old church, having orders to give instant alarm in case of danger by the ringing of the several bells. Silver-haired men, bending beneath the weight of years, alone passed along the deserted streets, and augured of the future in the now silent Plaza. The stores were closed, and anxiously the few Americans awaited the result; rising at dawn with the belief that ere twilight closed again their suspense would be terminated. On the morning of the 28th the booming of distant artillery was borne on the southern breeze. With throbbing hearts the inhabitants gathered about their doors, and strained their eyes toward the south. A large body of Mexicans, availing themselves of the cover of night, sallied from the Alamo, hoping to cut off a squad of ninety-two men, who leaving the main body of the Texan army, had advanced for the purpose of reconnoitring, and were posted at the old Mission of Conception, some two miles below the town; and here the contest was waged. The watchman on the church listened intently as each report reached his ear, and kept his fingers firmly on the bell-rope. An hour passed on, and the sun rode high in heaven; gradually the thundering died away. Quicker grew the breathing, and tighter the cold fingers clasped each other. The last sound ceased: a deathlike silence reigned throughout the town, and many a cheek grew colorless as marble. There came a confused sound of shouts—the mingling of many voices —the distant tramp of cavalry; and then there fell on the aching ears the deep, thrilling tones of the church bells.

An intervening bend in the river was quickly passed, and a body of Mexican cavalry dashed at full gallop across the plain, nor slackened their pace till secure behind the sombre walls of the Alamo.

At intervals of every few moments, small squads pushed in, then a running band of infantry, and lastly, a solitary horseman reeling in his saddle, dripping with gore. Madly his wounded horse sprang on, when just as the fort was gained, his luckless rider rolled senseless at the entrance. One deep groan was echoed from church to fortress. Victory, which had hovered doubtful o'er the bloody field, settled at last on the banner of the " Lone Star." Against what fearful odds is victory ofttimes won! The intrepid Texans, assaulted by forces which trebled their own, fought as only Texans can. With unerring precision they lifted their rifles, and artillerymen and officers rolled together in the dust. The brave little band conquered, and the flying Mexicans left them sole masters of the field of the "Horseshoe." On the hill which rose just beyond the town stood, in bold relief against the eastern sky, a tall square building, to which the sobriquet of " Powder-House " was applied. Here, as a means of increased vigilance, was placed a body of horse, for the purpose of watching the plain which stretched along the river. Fearing every moment to see the victorious Texans at the heels of their retreating infantry, they had orders to dash in, at the first glimpse of the advance-guard of the enemy. But night closed and none appeared, and, dreading the morning light, many lay down to sleep at the close of that eventful day. Several hours elapsed, and then the Texan forces, under General Burleson, wound across the valley, and settled along the verge of the town. The Alamo was beleaguered.

Forced, as it were, to remain a witness of the horrors of the then approaching conflict, the cousins strove to cast from them the gloomy forebodings which crept into their hearts, darkening the present and investing the future with phantoms of terror. Mrs. Carlton and Mary were far more hopeful than the remainder of the little circle, and kept up the semblance of cheerfulness, which ever flies at the approach of danger. The girls saw but little of the gentlemen, for Mr. Carlton was ever out in search of tidings from the camp, and Frank, in opposition to his sister's tearful entreaties, had enlisted immediately after General Burleson's arrival. His manner, during his brief visits, was considerate and kind; yet Mary fancied at times that he avoided her, though, marking her declining health, he had prescribed some simple remedy, and never failed to inquire if she were not improving. Still there was a certain something, indescribable, yet fully felt, which made her shrink from meeting him, and as week after week passed, her cheek grew paler, and her step more feeble.

With an anxious heart, Mrs. Carlton watched her failing strength; but to all inquiries and fears Mary replied that she did not suffer, save from her cough, and for a time dispelled her apprehensions.

One evening Mary stood leaning against the window, looking earnestly, wistfully upon the beautiful tints which ever linger in the western sky. She stretched her arms toward the dim outline, murmuring slowly:

"Oh! that my life may fade away as gently as those tints, and that I may at last rest on the bosom of my God."

Darkness closed around—the soft hues melted into the deep blue of the zenith as she stood communing with her own heart, and she started when a shawl was wrapped about her, and the window closed.

"As ministering physician, I cannot allow such neglect of injunctions. How dare you expose yourself after my express direction to keep close?"

"I have kept very close all day, and did not know that star-gazing was interdicted."

As she spoke, a violent fit of coughing succeeded; he watched her anxiously.

"Do you suffer any acute pain?"

"Occasionally I do; but nothing troubles me so much as an unpleasant fluttering about my heart, which I often have."

"You must be very careful, or your cough will increase as winter comes on."

Mary repressed a sigh which struggled up from her heart, and inquired if there was any news.

"We can not learn exactly what is happening within the Alamo, but feel assured the crisis is at hand; some excitement has prevailed in the garrison all day, and it is confidently expected in our camp that the assault will soon be made,"

"Oh! may God help you in the coming strife, and adjudge victory to the side of justice and liberty."

"Apparently the chances are against us, Miss Irving, yet I regard the future without apprehension, for the Texans are fearless, and General Burleson in every respect worthy the confidence reposed in him. Allow gloomy forebodings no room in your heart, but, like myself, anticipate a speedy termination of the war."

"Yet your situation is perilous in the extreme; hourly you incur danger, and each day may be your last. Oh! why will you hazard your life, and cause your sister such bitter anguish?" Mary replied, with quivering lips, while the tone faltered, despite her efforts to seem calm.

"At least, I could not die in a better cause; and as the price of independence, I would willingly yield up my life. Yet Ellen's tears are difficult to bear; I bade her adieu a few moments since, and must not meet her again till all is decided. So good-by, Miss Irving."

He held her hand in his, pressing it warmly, then lifted the cold fingers to his lips, and quietly turned away.

CHAPTER XX.

"It rains—what lady loves a rainy day?
She loves a rainy day who sweeps the hearth
And threads the busy needle, or applies
The scissors to the torn or thread-bare sleeve;
And blesses God that she has friends and home."
—*Anon.*

"MARY, where is your cousin? I have not seen her since breakfast," inquired Mrs. Carlton, as the two friends sat conversing in the chamber of the latter.

"She laid aside her book just now, declaring it was so dark she could scarcely read. This gloomy day has infected her spirits; she is probably in the dining-room. I will seek her." And rising, Mary left the apartment.

For two days the rain had fallen in torrents, and now on the third morning, the heavens were still overcast, and at intervals of every few moments the heavy clouds discharged themselves in copious showers. The despondency induced by the unsettled times was enhanced by the gloomy weather, and many an earnest wish was expressed that sunshine would soon smile again upon the town.

Weary with pacing up and down the dining-room, Florence had stationed herself at the window, and stood with her cheek pressed against the panes, gazing dreamily out upon the deluged streets. She was roused from her reverie by Mary's entrance.

"Florry, I have come in quest of you. Pray. how are you amusing yourself here, all alone?"

"Communing with my own thoughts, as usual. Here, Mary, stand beside me. As you came in I was puzzling myself to discover how those Mexican women across the street are employing themselves. They seem distressed, yet every now and then chatter with most perfect unconcern. There, they are both on their knees, with something like a picture hanging on the fence before them. They dart in and out of the house in a strange, excited manner. Perhaps you can enlighten me?"

Mary looked earnestly in the direction indicated by her cousin, and at length replied:

"You will scarcely credit my explanation: yet I assure you I perfectly understand the pantomine. Florry, look more particularly at the picture suspended in the rain. What does it most resemble, think you?"

"Ah, I see now—it is an image of the Virgin! But I should suppose they considered it sacrilegious to expose it to the inclemencies of the weather."

"Look closely, Florry, they are praying to the Virgin, and imploring a cessation of the rain. I once happened at Señor Gonzale's during a thunderstorm, and, to my astonishment, the family immediately hung out all the paintings of saints they possessed. I inquired the meaning, and was told in answer, that the shower would soon pass over, as they had petitioned the images to that effect. Those women have repeated a certain number of aves, and withdrawn into the house, but ere long you will see them return, and go through the same formula."

"It is almost incredible that they should ascribe such miraculous power to these little bits of painted canvas," replied Florence, gazing curiously upon the picture which was suspended with the face toward her.

"No, not incredible, when you remember the quantity of relics annually exported from Rome, such as ' chips of the Cross,' ' bones of the Apostles,' and ' fragments of the Virgin's apparel,' which Papists conscientiously believe are endowed with magical powers sufficient to relieve various infirmities. I doubt not that those women confidently expect a favorable response to their petition; and if such intercession could avail, it was certainly never more needed. Absurd as the practice appears to us, a doubt of the efficacy of their prayers never crosses their minds. They are both devout and conscientious."

"But, Mary, such superstitious ignorance is entirely confined to the degraded and uneducated classes. No really intelligent mind could rely on yonder picture to dispel these clouds, and win a ray of sunshine. I think you are too hasty in supposing that the enlightened portion of the Catholic Church place such implicit confidence in images and relics."

"What do you term the enlightened portion of

the church? Would not its prelates be considered as belonging to that class?"

"Most certainly they would, Mary: for doubtless many of the greatest minds Europe has produced, were and are still to be found among the Roman Catholic clergy. Yet you would not insinuate that these rely on the efficacy of such mummery as that we have just witnessed?" replied Florence, fixing her eyes inquiringly upon her cousin's face.

"Allow me to ask one question ere I reply, Florry, do you believe the days of miracles have passed away, or do you suppose that the laws of nature are still constantly infringed, the harmony of cause and effect destroyed, and wonderful phenomena still vouchsafed to favored Europeans?"

"Of course I do not advocate the theory that miracles occur at the present day. It is too preposterous to advance in this enlightened age. There are prehaps natural phenomena, only to be explained by scientific research; yet in the common acceptation of the term miracle, I unhesitatingly declare that I believe none have occurred since the days of Christ and the Apostles."

"Then, Florry, your position is untenable, for Romish prelates of the present day do most unquestionably defend the theory of the annual occurrence of miracles. Bishop ——, whose intellectual endowments are the constant theme of encomiums, has recently visited Italy. On his return to America, he brought with him a valuable collection of relics, which he distributed among the members of his church. Florry, I can vouch for the truth of what I now say. He declared himself extremely fortunate in having happened at Naples during the anniversary of the death of St. Janarius. Said he, ' I repaired to the place of his martyrdom, and took into my own hand the vial containing the blood of the blessed saint, now decomposed. As the hour rolled around I watched the holy dust in breathless anxiety; at the appointed moment I perceived a change in its appearance, and while I held the vial in my hand the ashes liquefied and became veritable blood! while the dark spots on a neighboring stone turned of a deep crimson.' Now the bishop related this miracle far and wide, and priests ministering at the altar repeated his words to their listening flocks. Sanctioned by the example of their prelates, do you wonder that the ignorant masses of the Romish church should implicity rely upon the intercession of saints, and place unbounded confidence in the miraculous powers imputed to relics? Again, the Manuals placed in the hands of the laity, are compiled under the special supervision of these ecclesiastical professors, who necessarily indorse all we see there advanced. In the Ursuline Manual I find this assertion: ' The Hail Mary was composed in Heaven, dictated by the Holy Ghost, and delivered to the faithful by the Angel Gabriel!' Now, Florry, does not this seem blasphemy, bordering on the absurd? What conscientious, honest, enlightened Christian would unblushingly defend such a declaration?"

"But, Mary, admitting as you do, that you believe there exist many truly conscientious members of this sect, why indulge your apprehension at the promulgation of its tenets?" replied Florence.

"I might answer you, Florry, in the words of Henry IV., who inquired of a celebrated Protestant divine, 'if a man might be saved by the Roman Catholic religion?' 'Undoubtedly,' replied the clergyman, 'if his life and heart be holy.' 'Then,' said the king, 'according to both Catholics and Protestants, I may be saved by the Catholic religion; but if I embrace your religion, I shall not be saved according to the Catholics.' Thus Henry most unquestionably adjudged Protestants the more tolerant of the two sects. Here, Florry, you have the clew to my anti-Romanism. I fear the extension of papal doctrines, because liberty of conscience was never yet allowed where sufficient power was vested in the Roman Catholic clergy to compel submission. To preserve the balance of power in ecclesiastical affairs is the only aim of Protestants. We but contend for the privilege of placing the Bible in the hands of the masses—of flashing the glorious flambeau of truth into the dark recesses of ignorance and superstition—into the abysmal depths of papal iniquity. Unscrupulously employing every method conducive to the grand end of disseminating Romish dogmas, the fagot, the wheel, and all the secret horrors of the Inquisition, were speedily brought to bear upon all who dared to assume the **privilege of worshiping God** according to the dictates of an unfettered conscience. If the bloody tragedies of the middle ages are no longer enacted upon the theatre of a more enlightened world, it is because the power so awfully abused has been wrested from the scarlet-robed tenants of the Vatican. The same fierce, intolerable tyranny is still exercised where their jurisdiction is unquestioned. From the administration of the pontifical states of Italy to the regulation of convent discipline, we trace the workings of the same iron rule. No barriers are too mighty to be overborne, no distinctions too delicate to be thrust rudely aside. Even the sweet sacredness of the home circle is not exempt from the crushing, withering influence. Ah! how many fair young members of the household band have been decoyed from the hearthstone and immured in gloomy cells. Ah! how many a widowed parent has mourned over the wreck of all that was beautiful in a cherished daughter, snatched by the hand of bigotry from her warm embrace, and forever incarcerated in monastic gloom. Oh! tell me, Florry, if compulsory service is acceptable to all-seeing God? If the warm young heart, beating behind many a convent grate, yearns to burst asunder the iron bands which enthrall her, and, mingling again upon the stage of life to perform the duties for which she was created, oh! where in holy writ is sanction found for the tyrannical decree which binds her there forever—a living sacrifice?"

CHAPTER XXI.

"Tis the light that tells the dawning
Of the bright millennial day,
Heralding its blessed morning,
With its peace-restoring ray.
* * * * *
"Man no more shall seek dominion
Through a sea of human gore;
War shall spread its gloomy pinion
O'er the peaceful earth no more."
—*Burleigh.*

IT was a dark, tempestuous night in December, and the keen piercing blasts whistled around the corners and swept moaningly across the Plaza. Silence reigned over the town. No sound of life was heard—the shout of laughter, the shriek of pain or wail of grief was stilled. The voices of many who had ofttimes hurried along the now silent and deserted streets were hushed in death. The eventful day had dawned and set, the records of its deeds borne on to God by the many that had fallen. Oh! when shall the millennium come? When shall peace and good-will reign throughout the world? When shall hatred, revenge, and malice die! When shall the fierce, bitter strife of man with fellow-man be ended? And oh! when shall desolating war forever cease, and the bloody records of the past be viewed as monster distortions of a maddened brain? These things shall be when the polity of the world is changed. When statesmen cease their political, and prelates their ecclesiastical intrigues; when monarch, and noble, and peasant, alike cast selfishness and dissimulation far from them; when the Bible is the text-book of the world, and the Golden Rule observed from pole to pole.

The 11th of December is marked with a white stone in the calendar of the Texans. During the fortnight which elapsed from the engagement of Conception, the Alamo had been closely invested by General Burleson, and brief though bloody struggles almost daily occurred. The besiegers numbered only eight hundred, while the fortress was garrisoned by twenty-five hundred Mexican troops. Yet well-directed valor has ever proved more than a match for numerical superiority. On the morning of the 11th a desperate assault was made, a violent struggle ensued, and ere long victory declared for the " Lone Star." With unutterable chagrin General Cos was forced to dispatch a messenger bearing the white banner of submission to the Texan commander, and night saw the Alamo again in Texan hands, and General Cos and his disheartened band prisoners of war.

Dr. Bryant had received, during the engagement, a wound in the arm, which he caused to be dressed, and placing the injured member in a sling, strove to soothe the dying and relieve the wounded. Early he dispatched tidings of his safety to his anxious sister, and now devoted himself to the suffering soldiery.

Midnight found him beside the couch of pain, and even as he bent to administer a sedative, a hand was lightly laid on his shoulder. Looking up, Frank perceived the muffled form of a female, though unable to determine who stood beside him, for the face was entirely concealed by a mantilla.

"Can I do any thing for you, Señora?"

"Dr. Bryant, will you leave your people here to see a dying Mexican—one who fell fighting against you?"

"Most assuredly, if I can render relief: but Inez, you should not have ventured here on such an errand; could no messenger be found? It was imprudent in you to come at this hour."

"No matter; I felt no fear of your people, and mine would not molest me. But I have little time to wait. Mañuel is sorely wounded: we bore him from the Alamo, and he lies at my father's. Can you do nothing for him?"

"I hope it is not too late to render assistance; we will go immediately." And drawing his cloak over the wounded arm, he followed her to Don Garcia's. Neither spoke till they reached the threshold; then Frank said:

"Inez, does Mañuel know you came for me?"

"Yes; he objected at first, but as the pain grew more acute, he begged us to do something for him. I told him there was none to help save you. He frowned a little, but nodded his head, and then I lost no time."

They entered the apartment of the sufferer, and

Inez started at the change which had taken place during her temporary absence. Mañuel feebly turned his head as the door opened, and his eyes brightened as they rested on Inez. He motioned her to sit beside him, and she complied, lifting his head and carefully leaning it upon her bosom. Dr. Bryant examined the wound, felt the pulse and stooping over him, asked:

"Nevarro, do you suffer much?"

Mañuel laid his hand on the bleeding side, and feebly inclined his head.

"Inez, I can only use one hand, will you assist me in binding this wound?"

She attempted to rise, but Nevarro clutched her hand and gasped—"Too late—too late!"

Resolved to do something, if possible, for his relief, Frank beckoned to the Don, who stood near, and with some difficulty they succeeded in passing a bandage round the mouth of the wound. The groans of the dying man caused even the cheek of the fearless Inez to blanch. She who scorned danger, and knew not fear, could not witness without a pang the sufferings of another. She moaned in very sympathy, and stroked gently back the straight raven hair, now clotted with blood. The exertion necessarily made proved fatal; the breathing grew short and painful, the pulse slow and feeble. Appealing was the look which the wounded one bent on Inez; he strove to utter his wishes, but alas, it was indeed too late. The blood gushed anew from his side, crimsoning bandage and couch, and dyeing

Inez's dress. Dr. Bryant took one of the cold hands and pressed it kindly. Mañuel opened his eyes, and looked gratefully on one who had at least endeavored to relieve him. Convulsively the fingers closed over his physician's hand; again he turned his face to Inez, and with a groan expired.

Frank took the lifeless form from her arms, and laying it gently back upon the pillow, closed the eyes forever, and covered the face.

No words save " Holy Mary!" escaped the Don's lips, as he quitted the room of death.

Inez's lips quivered, and the convulsive twitching of her features plainly indicated her grief at this mournful parting with the playmate of her youth—with her affianced husband. Yet the large dark eyes were undimmed; and her tone calm, as though the " King of Terrors " were not there in all his gloom.

" Inez, I sympathize with you in this affliction, and sincerely regret that the fatal wound was inflicted by one of my nation. Yet the past is irretrievable, though painful, and many are, like you, bereft of friends and relatives. Inez, in your hours of gloom and sadness can you not think of your reunion with Mañuel, where death and parting are unknown ?"

She had averted her head, and a look of unutterable bitterness rested on the pale, stern face.

" I thank you for coming, though you could not give Mañuel relief. It was good and kind in you to try, and none but Frank Bryant would have done it: again I thank you. I shall not forget this night, and you, Señor, shall be requited. I trust you are not suffering with your arm; why is it bound up?" And she laid her hand softly on it.

"I received a slight though rather painful wound during the engagement, and placed it in a sling for convenience and relief; but, Inez, it is well-nigh day, see how the stars are waning. You need rest, so good-night, or rather morning; I will see you again to-morrow." And Frank sought his sister, knowing full well her anxiety, and wishing speedily to allay it.

CHAPTER XXII.

> "Where is the place of meeting?
> At what hour rises the moon?
> I repair to what? to hold a council in the dark
> With common ruffians leagued to ruin states!"
> —*Byron.*

THE fierce storm of war had swept over the town, and quiet seemed succeeding. No sound of strife disturbed the stillness which settled around. Many had fallen, and the grass began to bud on the grave of Mañuel; no tear moistened the sod beneath which he rested. Inez often stood beside the newly-raised mound with folded arms, and a desolate, weary look on her beautiful features, which too plainly indicated a longing to sleep near him. Yet she never wept; for her love for Nevarro had been that of a cousin, perhaps not so fervent. Still, now that his steps no longer echoed at their door, and his deep voice sounded not again on her ear, a lonely feeling stole into her heart, and often she crept from her dreary home and sought the church-yard.

Christmas had come and gone; a joyless season to many saddened hearts accustomed to hail it with delight. The cousins had returned to their home, and were busily arranging their yard, and making some alterations for the New Year. Florence had begun of late to grow cheerful again, and Mary watched, with silent joy, the delicate tinge come back to her marble cheek. She seemed very calm, and almost hopeful; and the spirit of peace descended and rested on their hearth. Only one cause of sorrow remained—Mary's declining health: yet she faded so gently, and almost painlessly, that their fears were ofttimes lulled.

Dr. Bryant was still engaged in nursing the wounded, and only came occasionally, regretting often that it was not in his power to see them more frequently. A change had come over him of late; the buoyancy of his spirits seemed broken, and his gay tone of raillery was hushed; the bright, happy look of former days was gone, and a tinge of sadness was sometimes perceptible on his handsome face. Mrs. Carlton had spoken on her last visit of Frank's departure. She said she hoped he would return soon, as his business required attention at home. He would not leave, however, as long as his services were in requisition.

One Sabbath morning Inez attended mass—something unusual for her of late, for since Nevarro's death she had secluded herself as much as possible. She knelt in her accustomed place, with covered head, seemingly rapt in devotion, but the eyes rested with an abstracted expression on the wall beside her: her thoughts were evidently wandering from her rosary, and now and then the black brows met as her forehead wrinkled; still the fingers slid with mechanical precision up and down the string of beads. The services were brief, and the few who had assembled quietly departed As Inez rose to go, the Padre, who was hastening down the aisle, was stopped by a Mexican in the garb of a trader. They stood quite near, and the hoarse whisper of the latter fell on her listening ear.

" Meet me at the far end of the Alameda, when the moon rises to-night."

" I will be there before you: is there any good news ?"

A finger was laid on the lip, and a significant nod and wink were not lost upon the maiden, who, bowing low before the Padre, walked slowly away. The day wore on, much as Sabbaths ordinarily do, yet to her it seemed as though darkness would never fall again, and many times she looked out on the shadows cast by the neighboring houses athwart the street. Twilight closed at last, and having placed her father's evening meal before him, she cautiously gazed down the narrow alley, and perceiving no one stirring, sallied forth. The stars gave a faint light, and she hurried on toward the bridge: swift was her step, yet noiseless, and she glided on like a being from another world, so stealthy were her movements. The bridge was gained at length and almost passed, when she descried in the surrounding gloom a dark figure approaching from the opposite direction. Closer she drew the mantle about her form, and slackened her rapid pace. They met, and the stranger paused and bent eagerly forward:

"Who goes there?"

The voice was well known. Inez's heart gave a quick bound, and she answered:

"Inez de Garcia!"

"Why, where are you roaming to this dark night, Inez? Are you not afraid to venture out alone and so far from home?"

"No, Doctor, I have no fears; I was never a coward, you know; and besides, who would harm me, an unoffending woman? Surely your people will not molest me?"

"No, certainly not. But, Inez, I hope you are not bending your steps toward the Alamo?"

"I am a friend to the Americans, though they have taken the last of my family there was to give. Yet I will be true to Mary and to you. Fear nothing for me and let me pass on my errand."

He stood aside. "Bueño noche, Señorita."

"Bueño noche;" and she glided on. "I fear I have lost time;" and hastily glancing toward the east, she saw a faint light stealing up from the horizon. Redoubling her speed she pushed on, but, despite her efforts, the moon rose with uncommon brilliance as she approached the place of rendezvous, and soon every object was bathed in a flood of light.

The Alameda, which she had just entered, was a long double row of majestic cotton-woods, which, stretching out in the direction of the Powder-House, was the favorite promenade with the inhabitants of the town. Previous to the breaking out of the war numbers were to be seen here every afternoon, some walking, others playing games, another group dancing, and the graver portion of the company resting on the rude seats supplied for the purpose. But their favorite resort was blood-stained, for the Alameda was the battle-field in the late desperate conflict, and the smooth surface was torn and trampled by the stamp of prancing cavalry. Dark spots were still visible, that were yet damp with gore. Just to the west rose the grim walls of the fort, distinctly seen through the opening between the trees. Beyond where the avenue ceased, stood a low irregular building of stone, thatched with tule.

Inez stood at the threshold and listened intently. The place bore a desolate air, and neither sound nor light betokened the presence of a human being. It had long been uninhabited, and some declared it was haunted, so that the Padre had some time before sprinkled holy water profusely about, in order to drive away the evil one.

Cautiously Inez tried the fastening; it swerved not beneath her firm, strong grasp. She shook it slightly; a hollow echo answered back. Entrance was impossible; and even as she lingered irresolute, the sound of approaching steps was borne to her listening ears by the night wind. What should she do? Without a moment's hesitation she glided swiftly to a cluster of chapperal, and crouched low among its thorny branches. Inez had scarcely secreted herself, when the figure of a man, directing his steps to the house she had just left, warned her to keep quiet. He stood still a moment, then knocked. Drearily the knock resounded through the empty building. Again was the signal for admission given, but no response greeted the anxious tympanums.

"Why in the name of twenty devils don't you open the door?" and he shook it violently: still no answer.

"I swear I'll batter it down, and stretch you on it to boot, if you don't let me in. Why do you keep me waiting? I am too late already."

"Nay, nay; restrain your impatience," said a voice behind him.

"By the saints, you are come in good time, Padre. I had well-nigh made a soldier's entrance."

"No need of violence, Señor. Why could not you wait in Christian patience?"

"Look here, my good friend. I come not all the way from Mexico to listen to a lecture; and you will do well to save your canting for a better time and a worse man. So, Mazzolin, just open the door of this cursed den."

Roused by the bold language of the stranger, the Padre, though anxious to learn his errand, was still true to his policy, and could in no measure compromise the dignity of his person.

"There is no obligation resting on me to do so against my will, and no man shall bully or threaten me, a priest of our holy church." He had partially opened the door, but closed it again.

Enraged beyond degree, the soldier grasped what little collar was afforded by the habit he wore.

"You infernal, canting hypocrite! I swear by Cortes I'll kick you to a jelly—I'll bastinade you till you won't know the Virgin from the Devil, if you don't instantly let me in, and keep your lying tongue in your Jesuit head. Think you to gull me with your holy talk? I know you all: you are a blessed, holy brotherhood, truly. Have I not seen your letters to Mexico, you canting scoundrel?" He shook the Padre violently as he delivered this benediction.

Now Father Mazzolin, like many of his sex, was fond of supporting his dignity, and reverence for his sacred person was especially inculcated by his teachings. Yet when firmly met his threats melted away, and, to all appearances, his choler too; for he knew full well when to succumb and when to oppose belligerent demonstrations. The expression of rage that darkened the face of the soldier, left no doubt that he would execute his threat if further opposed. And Father Mazzolin, fully satisfied that the organ of reverence was altogether omitted in his cranium, thought it best to comply.

"Ha! you can understand Irish logic as well as

the next brave one." And he entered, followed by the Padre, who ground his teeth with mortification.

An hour later they stood again on the threshold in earnest converse, not perceiving the dark form which fled, on the reopening of the door, to the old hiding-place. They turned to go in different directions: the stranger stopped, and calling to the Padre, desired him to keep well the secret, and in no way divulge a breath of their conference.

"It could not be in safer hands," was answered back, and they parted.

A low, bitter laugh escaped Inez's lips as, waiting till it was safe to venture forth, she rose from the chapperal and hastened homeward.

"Padre, cunning though you are, we are well mated, there are few like unto you and me."

CHAPTER XXIV.

"I simply tell thee peril is at hand,
And would preserve thee!"
—*Byron.*

Two days later the cousins sat in their front room, Florence intently reading, Mary watching beside the couch of pain, bathing her aunt's brow, and chafing the hands. Aunt Lizzy was suffering from violent nervous headache: all day she had tossed restlessly about, and now, soothed by the gentle touches on her brow, had fallen asleep. Her fingers had tightly clasped Mary's small, thin hands, but gradually relaxing their hold, sunk beside her. Softly smoothing back the disordered hair, the young nurse failed to perceive the entrance of Dr. Bryant, and only looked up when a beautiful bouquet of flowers was laid upon her lap. The feverish glow deepened on her cheek as she warmly thanked him.

"I am glad you like them, Miss Irving."

"How could I do otherwise ?"

" My bunch is equally beautiful," cried Florence, holding it up for inspection. " Pray, Doctor, how came you so thoroughly acquainted with our different tastes ? You have selected admirably."

" I am gratified at succeeding so happily in my arrangement of them. But I hope your aunt is not seriously indisposed ?"

" No, merely a bad nervous attack, to which she is subject."

" Miss Mary as you are free from apprehension on her account. can you take a short ride this evening? I have a gentle horse at the gate, and if you will trust yourself with me, I think a good canter will benefit you exceedingly: will you go?"

Mary sought Florence's eye; it brightened with pleasure.

"Certainly, Mary; why do you hesitate ? I am very glad Dr. Bryant suggested it; I will take good care of aunt. and the ride will doubtless benefit you."

"You are very kind, Doctor; I will only detain you while I change my dress." And she withdrew.

"Don't you think she looked much better to-day?" asked Florence anxiously, as her cousin left the room.

"She has certainly more color, but I am afraid it is only a feverish glow. Let me entreat you, Miss Hamilton, to watch over her with the greatest care: the slightest exposure might cause a return of that terrible cough, and in her feeble state I fear for the consequences."

'She has grown very, very thin, within the last month; but then, when warm weather comes again, I doubt not she will grow rosy and strong once more.' They both sighed heavily, as though against conviction each had striven to cheer the other.

Mary re-entered the room equipped for her ride, and now, for the first time, Florence thought her cousin beautiful. Beneath her straw hat floated back from her fair face a luxuriant mass of brown curls; a bright blush mantled the delicate cheek, and the gentle blue eyes seemed unusually large and brilliant. A smile dimpled round her lip as she met the fond glance bent upon her. Florence tenderly clasped her hand a moment, then kissed her warmly, and bade Dr. Bryant take all care of her. He promised to do so, and soon they had passed beyond her sight. They rode slowly, lest Mary should be too much fatigued; and often the eyes of her companion rested on the frail but lovely being by his side.

"Which way shall we ride?"

"If you have no preference, suppose we go to San Pedro?"

"You could not have selected more in accordance with my own wishes."

A long silence ensued, broken only by the clatter of their horses' hoofs along the gravel path.

"The prospect of leaving forever these beautiful environs, which I have so often admired, fills me with inexpressible regret. My heart clings to San Antonio, though my residence here has been very brief!" said Dr Bryant, sadly.

"Do you go to return no more?" asked Mary, with averted head.

"Yes, most probably I shall never see this place again; for I wish to visit Europe so soon as my business affairs are arranged at home, and on my return, shall devote myself to my profession." He fixed his eyes earnestly on her face as he spoke.

Slowly the head drooped, till the hat concealed her features.

"We shall miss you very much when you are gone. Florry and I feel deeply grateful for your continued kindness, and never—no, never shall we forget your care of my uncle."

"Take care—take care; you are dropping your reins."

He gathered them up, and replaced them in her hand.

"Thank you; I had quite forgotten them."

"Do you not think it would be best for you and

Florence to return to your friends in Louisiana? This is an unpleasant home for you."

"It was my uncle's wish that we should remain here, and I know Florry would not consent to leave, unless some danger threatened. We have learned to love San Antonio more dearly than any other place, except our old home;" replied Mary, earnestly.

"By-the-by, I had almost forgotten to mention that I have had a letter from an old friend, who inquired very particularly after you—Dudley Stewart; you knew him, I think, in New Orleans. His letter is dated six months ago; but I am happy to receive it at all during these unsettled times."

"We heard of his marriage," said Mary, in a low tone, as the image of Florence rose before her.

"His marriage! Oh, no! you must be mistaken. He would most certainly have mentioned it, for we are old and intimate friends."

"It was reported that he had married his cousin."

"Ah! is that all? I am not much surprised that you should have heard that, for before I left home it was quite current. His widowed mother was very anxious to make the match; but Stewart assured me he would never comply with her wishes, as he had fully resolved never to wed a woman he did not tenderly love; and though quite pretty, Ellen is not sufficiently intellectual to attract such a man."

"Are you quite sure of this, Dr. Bryant?" said Mary, in a quick, eager tone.

"Certainly; I had it from his own lips."

"Oh! I—'" She stopped short, and her cheek crimsoned, as she met the piercing glance of his dark eye bent upon her face. Her small hands trembled so that the reins quivered, and she closed her eyes for a moment, while the glow fled from her cheeks, leaving them pale as marble.

He caught her hand, and steadied her in her saddle.

"Forgive my inattention, Miss Irving, you are not strong enough to extend your ride. Your face is very pale, and you look fatigued."

"Yes, let us go home—home." Her voice was low and faltering, and she with difficulty restrained the tears which sprung to her eyes.

They turned their horses' heads, and neither attempted to remove the restraint which both experienced. They entered the town, and then seeing her hands glide quickly to her side, he gently said:

"I am afraid we are riding too fast for you."

Her lips writhed for a moment with acute pain; but with a faint smile, which touched him with its sadness, she replied:

"I am better now—the pain has almost left me. I am very sorry to trouble you so much, Dr. Bryant."

"Trouble!" he murmured, as if communing with his own heart. "I see you do not know me, nor ever will; for none have truly read my soul or sympathized." A look of bitterness passed over his face, and a sterner expression rested there than Mary had ever marked before. She knew not what to reply, for she could **not** comprehend the change, and even as she pondered, he pointed to the western sky, and, much in his usual tone, asked:

"Don't you think the sunsets here exceed any you ever beheld elsewhere?"

"In brilliancy they certainly do. Yet I love still better the soft tints which often linger till the stars come out. I think they blend and harmonize more beautifully with the deep blue of the zenith than any I have seen before, and I have watched sunsets from my childhood."

"You are right; I have noticed in more northern latitudes a very perceptible difference in the appearance of the firmament. The moon, for instance, on cold, clear nights, presents a silvery, glittering disc, but the soft mellow light of a southern clime is wanting."

While he spoke, the figure of a woman emerged from a house near by, and, softly approaching Mary's horse, laid her finger on her lips, and, pressing a piece of paper into her hand, returned as silently as she came. Dr. Bryant turned his head toward Mary as he finished speaking, and, catching a glimpse of the retreating form, looked inquiringly at her.

"I believe it was Inez, though the face was entirely concealed. She did not speak, but gave me this paper," and Mary unrolled the note.

"Marinita,

"Santa Anna has crossed the Rio Grande with eight thousand men. I warn you of your danger.

You can get horses now, for the Padre can not control your people. There are brave men in the Alamo, tell them of their danger. Again I say, fly quickly from San Antonio.   INEZ."

With a groan, Mary handed him the paper. In silence he perused and returned it to her.

"Tell me, was it Inez who warned you before?"

"Yes, she told me we incurred unknown dangers by remaining here." He mused for several moments.

"Ah! I can understand it all now. Several nights ago, returning from the Alamo, I met her on the bridge alone; she seemed excited, I thought, and impatient at meeting me, for I questioned her rambling so late."

"Inez is a warm friend, and what she advises I feel almost bound to do, for she is not timid, and only real danger rouses her apprehension."

"Eight thousand men! and not two hundred to man the Alamo. Inez is right; this is not a proper place for you. We will go, as we once decided, to Washington; and when you are in safety, I will return and lend my efforts to the feeble garrison."

They reached the gate, and he gently lifted the frail form from the saddle; and, drawing her arm through his led her to the house. As they entered, he bent his head and said, in a low tone:

"Tell me candidly, are you able to undergo the fatigue incident to this journey? I fear you are not."

"Yes, I shall perhaps grow stronger; at any rate, if you do not change your mind, let no fears for me influence you."

When leaving, he said it was probable that all would be in readiness for their departure within a couple of days, as he wished to see them secure, and then return.

"Mrs. Carlton will accompany us when she learns this terrible news?" said Mary, inquiringly.

"Oh yes; I can not consent for her to remain, and besides, Mr. Carlton has been anxious for some time regarding his family."

Florence, having read the note, fully approved their promptly removing, and all necessary preparations were made for immediate departure.

Mary longed inexpressibly to impart to her cousin what she had learned respecting Mr. Stewart, but shrank instinctively from reviving hopes which might never be realized—hopes which Florence had long since crushed and cast out of her heart as dead. With an earnest prayer that her cousin might yet be blessed and happy, Mary determined not to broach the subject, at least for a time. Dr. Bryant without delay apprised the garrison of the rumor which had reached him, and a courier was immediately dispatched to head-quarters for reinforcements sufficient to defend this important fortress—this key of the state—from the powerful force now advancing to assault it. Horses were supplied with alacrity, for he had made many and warm friends, and two large tents, together with a baggage-wagon, were readily granted to one who so nobly contributed to the relief of the sick, wounded and dying.

At length every arrangement was completed, and the next morning appointed for their departure. Aunt Lizzy had objected at first, but speedily became reconciled when Dr. Bryant painted, in a graphic manner, the horrors which were about to ensue.

As the shades of evening came gently on, the girls set out for Mrs. Carlton's, as from her dwelling they commenced their journey. Aunt Lizzy remained to give some final direction, and then came a sorrowful parting with their servants, one of whom took Mary in her arms and bade God bless her, while the tears rolled over her wrinkled face. Mary could not repress her own, and she sobbed convulsively. Dr. Bryant, who had come over for them, laid his hand on the shoulder of the true-hearted negress, and said:

"Why, Aunt Fanny, you must not excite Miss Irving; she is not strong, you know, and has a long ride before her to-morrow."

"Oh yes, Doctor, it will do well enough for you to tell me not to cry, but I can't help it, for I love her as if she was my own child, and if I thought to see her again I should not grieve so much; but I saw her mother before her, and I know how she grew pale and thin, and then took to the sofa, and never rose up till she was carried to her grave; and can't I see that blessed child going just like her? Oh! it's no use talking to me; she ain't long for this world, and it's hard—yes it's hard for her to die away from old Fanny!" and she covered her face with her apron, and sobbed aloud.

Mary wiped her own tears quickly away, and taking the hand of her old friend, led her back to the kitchen. For several moments her companions waited anxiously for her; and soon she advanced slowly to meet them. Frank drew her arm through his, and sadly they walked away. Passing the gate, Mary paused and looked out on the river, where she had so often sat at this hour; and sad though sweet associations, infinite in number, crowded upon her mind.

How calm and beautiful all nature seemed, as though arrayed in its loveliest garb to claim her affection, that, in after years, the memory of that western home might steal gently up amidst surrounding gloom, to charm away the anguish of some bitter hour, and soothe the saddened spirit. Her heart was inexpressibly touched, and she averted her head to conceal the expression of keen sorrow which rested on her face.

"This view of the San Antonio has often struck me as particularly fine," said Dr. Bryant, turning to Florence, whose pale cheek alone attested regret at leaving her home.

"Yes, I know none superior; and our favorite ramble was along this bank, and down the river side."

"Its windings are multitudinous, yet how graceful every curve: and then, the deep blue of its waters adds not a little to the beauty of the whole. But we have not leisure to admire it now, for your cousin must not be chilled, and the wind blows freshly from the north."

He stepped on as he spoke, but feeling the small hands clasped over his arm, looked earnestly down into the pale face at his side. Mary was bending a last, long look on house and tree and river; as they walked on the different objects passed beyond her view, and then a faint moan escaped her lips. She met the anxious gaze of her friend, and replied to its silent questioning:

"Forgive what doubtless seems a great weakness. You and Florry cannot sympathize with me now. You will both return ere long, but my eyes have rested for the last time on each loved object. I have dreaded this parting from the home that has grown so dear to me—but the pang is over."

Her deep blue eyes rested on his face, and touchingly sad was the expression, as she swept back the clustering hair from her brow. The lips quivered, as of late they often did when she was excited. Florence did not hear her words, for she had crossed the street; but Frank's heart throbbed violently as he listened to her low, sad tone. Laying his hand on hers, that were tightly clasped, he pressed them gently, and said, in a slightly faltering voice:

"For Florence's sake—for mine—for your own, do not give way to such gloomy forebodings! Your depressed spirits will act injuriously on your health. Let me beg you to place no confidence in Aunt

Fanny's words at parting; she was herself scarce conscious of their import."

"I have no gloomy forebodings, no apprehension of the future, and generally no depressed spirits; but I know full well that my life is gradually wasting away, slowly, gently, and almost without pain. I am sinking to an early tomb. Yet I would not have it otherwise if I could. Death has long since lost all terrors for me; I have no fear—all is peace and quiet. I am paining you. Forgive me, Dr. Bryant; but knowing that you and Florry were anxious about me I thought it best to tell you that I am fully aware of my danger, if so I can term what I would not avert."

A shudder crept over the strong man as he looked down at the calm, colorless face of her who spoke so quietly of death, and of quitting forever the scenes she loved so truly.

"I cannot—will not believe you are so ill. You will grow stronger when we leave this place, and a year hence, when quite well again, you will beg pardon for the pain you have given me."

A faint smile played round the thin lips, and in silence they proceeded to Mrs. Carlton's.

CHAPTER XXV.

"Who's here besides foul weather?"
—*Shakspeare.*

FAR away stretched the prairie, bounded, ocean-like, only by the horizon; the monotony occasionally relieved by clumps of aged live oaks, which tossed their branches to and fro in summer breezes and in wintry blasts, and lent a mournful cadence to the howlings of the tempest. Now and then a herd of deer, lifting proudly their antlered heads, seemed to scorn danger from the hand of man, as they roamed so freely over the wide, desolate waste which possessed no visible limits. And groups of cattle, starting at the slightest sound, tossed their horns in defiance, and browsed along the mesquit, in many places so luxuriant as well-nigh to conceal their forms. The day had been unusually warm for January, and the sun beamed down with a sickening intensity which made the blood tingle in the veins. Toward noon the sky assumed a dull, leaden cast, and light flakes of cloud, like harbingers of evil, scudded ominously overhead. The sun passed the zenith, and a low sighing breeze swept moaningly across the wide waste, even as the wail of lost spirits floats out on the midnight air, and then is hushed forever.

The cattle that stood leisurely cropping about, and now and then moving a few paces, lifted their heads, snuffed the air, and, with a simultaneous lowing, started at full speed to the timbered tracks, where they were wont to resort for shelter from the winds of winter. On, on they rushed, till in the distance one might fancy them a quantity of beetles, or other insects, dotting the surface before them. Soon not a vestige remained of the flying herd, and happy it was for them they made good their retreat, and gained a place of refuge ere the "norther" burst in all its keenness on the unprotected plain. Wildly the piercing blasts whistled through the trees, and rushed furiously on, unimpeded by the forest, which in more eastern lands present a formidable barrier to their progress. The rain began to fall heavily, when a small cavalcade sought the protection of a clump of oaks, by placing the leafy boughs between themselves and the beating, driving torrents. The party consisted of several ladies and gentlemen, two children, and as many servants! the latter in a wagon, the remainder on horseback. With all possible speed the gentlemen dismounted, and, tightly buttoning their great coats about them, proceeded to stretch two tents, by means of poles and pins, carried in the wagon.

Night closed in, and finding a sheltered spot beneath the trees, a large fire was kindled, which threw its ruddy light into the surrounding tents, and illumined the entire grove. The horses were picketed out, almost within reach from the tents, and the wagon containing their stores drawn so near as, in some degree, to shelter them. The servants prepared the evening meal—simple, it is true, yet enjoyed far more than a sumptuous repast of Indian delicacies and untold ragouts, eaten without the sauce of hunger produced by their long ride. More than a week had elapsed since leaving San Antonio, and Mary had borne better than they dared to hope the fatigue of the journey.

To-night, however, she lay exhausted on her pallet, the thin cheek bright with fever: gently she declined all that was proffered, and her hollow cough chased the smile from the lips of her friends. Dr. Bryant knelt beside her, and taking one hot hand in his own, asked, in a low, anxious voice, if she suffered.

Turning away her face, she said—"Oh no, not much. There is, however, such a painful throbbing about my heart I can scarcely breathe. Am I not feverish?" she continued.

"Yes;" and he placed his fingers on the pulse, beating violently. "I am afraid you have taken severe cold—the day has been so inclement." And, with a somewhat unsteady hand, he administered a potion.

"Don't feel uneasy about me, Doctor, I shall be better when I sleep." And she turned away, and wearily closed her eyes.

When the camp-fire burned low, and all slumbered save Mary, who could not calm her feverish excitement, and lay wide awake, she fancied she heard steps around the tent. All was silent; then again came the sound; and raising herself, she thought she perceived some one standing near the entrance.

The figure disappeared, and then followed a rumbling, stamping, kicking, as though the horses were verily bewitched. "The Indians!" thought Mary; and quickly rising, she threw a black mantle round her, and creeping to the door of the tent, peeped out. The horses still seemed restless, stamping and snorting, and she thought she could softly reach the adjoining tent and rouse the gentlemen, knowing that their arms were in readiness. She had just stepped out of her own tent, and stood out of doors, when she caught a glimpse of a dark, muffled figure walking toward her. The rain had ceased, but it was very dark, and only by the aid of the fire-light, now grown dim, she perceived it. A cold shudder crept over her, as, raising her eyes to the blackened sky but an instant, she sprang forward toward the place where she fancied the gentlemen were sleeping. A hand was laid on her arm and a deep voice sounded in her ear:

"Be not alarmed, Miss Mary, I am here!"

She trembled so that she could scarcely stand. He supported her a moment, ere she replied in a whisper—

"What causes the disturbance to-night?"

"I feel assured there are Indians about, though you need fear nothing, for they are not in sufficient number to attack us. There are four men in our party—nearly a dozen muskets, besides my pistols, and plenty of ammunition. Were you one of the timid sort, I should not venture to tell you my apprehensions: but I know that you are not. I have not slept, or even lain down; and a while ago, I heard the sound of hoofs approaching. Taking my pistols, I went round to the horses, and had not waited many moments before I saw two figures, evidently reconnoitring and planning the abduction of our horses, who seemed much alarmed. I suppose the intruders must have seen me, for they suddenly wheeled off and galloped away."

"Perhaps there is a party not far distant, for whose assistance they have gone."

"Possibly, though I think not; but you must not stand on this wet ground." He led her to the tent, and seating himself near the door, continued:

"I shall not sleep to-night, and rest assured you will be most carefully guarded. You were imprudent to venture out on such a night."

"What! when I thought there was danger, and none, save myself, aware of it?"

"Did you think I could rest, knowing, as I do, how you are suffering?"

"I never imagined you were up, or watching, for I heard no sound near me."

"Well, no matter; sleep, if you can, and dream of peace, and quiet, and perfect happiness." He sighed heavily as he spoke, and rising, renewed the fire.

Mary lay watching him as he paced to and fro in front of the burning logs—his arms folded across his chest, and his cap drawn over the brow: gradually a sense of utter weariness stole over her, and she slept.

At dawn a bustle commenced in the camp, and

preparation were made—first for breakfast, then for moving.

When Mary came out, her pale face and wearied look attracted Mrs. Carlton's attention.

"My dear child, I am afraid you are scarcely able to travel to-day; did you not sleep well?"

"Not so soundly as I could have wished," she said, passing her hand over her brow, as if to remove some painful thought.

Dr. Bryant acquainted them with the adventure of the night, suggesting, that in future some of the party should watch, as security for their horses; and all agreed that it was advisable.

"How readily one might suppose this a gypsy encampment. Miss Hamilton and myself are quite dark enough to favor the illusion, and Ellen and Mr. Carlton would pass as of gypsy descent; but what would they think of Miss Mary? She is decidedly anti-gypsy in her appearance."

"I can tell you, Uncle Frank," cried Elliot, clapping his hands; "they would take Miss Mary for an angel that came to our tent, like the one that came down to see Abraham."

"Unfortunately, angels never appear in the form of a lady, Elliot; so you must tax your ingenuity to dispose of me in a different manner," said Mary, smiling gently on the noble boy beside her.

"Indeed, I would sooner think you ought to be an angel than any gentleman I know, or lady either; don't you think so too, Uncle Frank?"

"Certainly I do; but, Elliot, you should not have

made me say so in Miss Florence's presence. You forget that she is also a young lady."

" No, I don't, uncle, and I ask her pardon if I was rude; but I heard you say Miss Mary was an angel, and though I like Miss Florence very much indeed, I can't help thinking so too."

Dr. Bryant's cheek flushed, and he glanced quickly at Mary. Mr. and Mrs. Carlton and Florence laughed good-naturedly; and laying his hand on the boy's head, Frank said:

"My very promising nephew, you will never be accused of want of candor if you grow up in your present spirit."

Mary drew the child to her, and whispered in his ear:

" Your uncle meant that I should soon be in Heaven, Elliot; and I hope it will not be very long before I am an angel. Don't you see how thin and pale I am ?"

Elliot's eyes filled, as he looked earnestly at the gentle girl, so wasted of late, and throwing his arms about her neck, he hid his face on her shoulder, and murmured:

"Oh! you must not go from us—we can't spare you even to God! Why does he want to take you? He has plenty of angels already around him! Mother and uncle and I had almost as soon die ourselves as see you go away forever."

None heard what passed between them; but Mrs. Carlton saw a look of pain on Mary's pure white brow, and gently drawing her son away, changed the conversation by asking if it would not be better for Mary to ride awhile in the wagon.

"I am afraid she would find the jolting rather too much for her. However, it will answer as a change, and by driving myself, I can avoid many inequalities. So, Miss Irving, make up your mind to relinquish your Babieca at least for to-day."

"You are very kind, Dr. Bryant, but I greatly prefer your riding as usual. Indeed you need not look so incredulous. I won't allow you to make such a sacrifice."

"I was not aware that I was making any sacrifice," he coldly answered, and turned away.

Mary's lips quivered with internal pain, but she offered no further opposition.

All was in readiness for moving on. Dr. Bryant stood arranging Florence's bridle, and bantering her on her inattention to the reins. She laughed in her turn.

"Indeed, Doctor, don't you think me a capital horsewoman? you will certainly admit it, after being vanquished in a race?"

"Really, Miss Florence, I rather think the credit due to your fine horse than to your skill as a rider."

"Ah, incorrigible as usual, I see, Doctor!" and she rode off to join Mr. Carlton.

Mr. Carlton had placed Mary in the wagon, and carefully arranged her shawls that she might rest easily. Frank quietly seated himself, and drove on.

"I shall not exert myself in the least to entertain you, so you need not expect it; for having very politely told me you did not desire my company, I shall not disturb you with my chatter, I promise you, and take this opportunity to inform you that my tympanums are at your service the remainder of the day."

He glanced over his shoulder at the frail form nearly buried beneath the weight of shawls and cloaks wrapt about her. She smiled, and laid her head on her arm: as she did so, he, looking at her, failed to perceive a large stone in the track, and the wheels passing directly over it, caused the wagon to jolt most unmercifully.

Florence was just in the rear, and, unable to control her mirth, laughed outright as Frank and Mary bounced up and down; and, riding up to them, merrily asked " if Mary duly appreciated her good fortune in having so careful and scientific a driver."

Not a little amused, yet scarce able to laugh, the latter replied that " she did indeed congratulate herself on the change of drivers, as she would not have survived the day had it been otherwise."

Frank joined heartily in their merriment.

" Miss Hamilton," said he, " if you only knew what caused me to overlook that unfortunate stone, you would be more lenient in your criticisms."

" I am very sure you will adduce every possible reason in your own favor, sir, and therefore feel no sympathy for your carelessness," she retorted.

" Really you make me out as incorrigible a self-excuser as the heroine of Miss Edgeworth's juvenile tales; though even she chanced upon a good excuse occasionally. Come, try me, and see what I can urge in my own defense."

"Well, then, I ask you, *à la Godfrey*, what you were thinking of when you, who had an ailing lady in your cart, drove directly over the largest rock you have seen in a week?"

"In the first place, I did not see it. You need not look quite so incredulous; I assure you I did not."

"That is very evident, but no excuse at all. Pray, where were your eyes?"

"Where nature intended them to be, I suppose."

"Nonsense! why didn't you use them?"

"Because I have not the faculty of looking two ways at once, like Brahma; and my optics were irresistibly drawn in an opposite direction."

"A truce to all such excuses!"

"Patience, Miss Florence, hear me only once more. The reason is, that I was looking at your cousin over there, and calculating the chances of her surviving suffocation."

"There is certainly some danger. Pray, Mary, why wrap up so closely? Æolus has closed the mouth of his cave, and the warring winds are securely pent in their prison."

"Are you not very much edified, Miss Mary? I should beg pardon for such a waste of time and talk, if I were not aware that

'A little nonsense now and then,
Is relished by the wisest men.' "

As Mary made no reply, he turned around and regarded her earnestly. Her hat had fallen back from the face, which rested on his black cloak. Every vestige of mirth fled from his countenance as they gazed on the sleeping girl. The feverish flush had left the cheek, now perfectly wan; the dark brown hair clung on the pure, beautiful brow, and beneath the closed eyes were dark circles, traced by mental suffering. The expression of the face was perfectly calm, yet a wearied look, as though longing to be at rest, lingered there. So motionless she lay, that Frank hastily placed his hand on hers to feel if warmth and vitality remained. Slowly and faint came the pulsations, and, as he watched her death-like slumber, his cheek grew pale, a look of unutterable anguish settled on his noble brow, and the finely cut lips were tightly compressed, as with some acute though hidden pain. Florence slowly returned to Mr. and Mrs. Carlton—no smile passed her lips the remainder of the day; she seemed now, for the first time, to realize her cousin's danger, and naught could divert her mind from this new grief.

Dr. Bryant bent his head upon his breast, and murmured in saddened tones: "Oh, Mary! Mary! how gladly would I give all I possess on earth to see you strong and well again."

CHAPTER XXVI.

> " And therefore my heart is heavy
> With a sense of unquiet pain,
> For but Heaven can tell if the parted
> Shall meet in the earth again.
>
> " With Him be the time and the season
> Of our meeting again with thee:
> Whether here, on these earthly borders,
> Or the shore of the world to be."
>
> —*Carey.*

ONE day our party had traveled further than on any previous occasion: long and tedious was the ride, still they pushed on, hoping to reach some stream ere the tents were pitched for the night, as an abundant supply of pure fresh water was essential to the comfort of their camp. In the metaphorical strain of a certain writer—"Phœbus drove his steeds to be foddered in their western stables." Slowly twilight fell upon the earth, and, one by one, the lamps of heaven were lit. The wagon in which Dr. Bryant and Mary rode was rather in the rear of the party, as the riders pressed anxiously forward. The cool-night wind blew fresh upon the fevered brow of the invalid, and gently lifted and bore back the clustering curls.

" I am very much afraid you will take cold:" and Dr. Bryant wrapped his cloak carefully about her.

" Thank you:" and she sank back in its heavy

folds, and looked up to the brilliant firmament, where the stars glittered, like diamonds on a ground of black velvet, in the clear, frosty air.

"Orion has culminated; and how splendidly it glows to-night, I think I never saw it so brilliant."

"Perhaps it appears so from the peculiar position whence you view it. You never observed it before from a wagon, in a broad prairie, with naught intervening between the constellation and yourself save illimitable space, though I agree with you in thinking it particularly splendid. I have ever regarded it as the most beautiful among the many constellations which girt the heavens."

"I have often wondered if Cygnus was not the favorite of papists, Dr. Bryant."

"Ah! it never occurred to me before, but, since you mention it, I doubt not they are partial to it. How many superstitious horrors are infused into childish brains by nurses and nursery traditions! I well remember with what terror I regarded the Dolphin, or, in common parlance, ' Job's Coffin,' having been told that, when that wrathful cluster was on the meridian, some dreadful evil would most inevitably befall all who ventured to look upon it; and often, in my boyhood, I have covered my face with my hands, and asked its whereabouts. Indeed I regarded it much as Æneas did Orion, when he says:

> 'To that blest shore we steered our destined way,
> When sudden dire Orion roused the sea!
> All charged with tempests rose the baleful star,
> And on our navy poured his watery war.'

The contemplation of the starry heavens has ever exerted an elevating influence on my mind. In viewing its glories, I am borne far from the puerilities of earth, and my soul seeks a purer and more noble sphere."

"Your quotation from Virgil recalled a passage in Job—, 'Seek him that maketh the seven stars and Orion, and turneth the shadow of death into morning.' Oh! how inimitably sublime is inspired language—and 'turneth the shadow of death into morning.' And how comforting the promise conveyed," said Mary, earnestly.

"Miss Irving, don't you admire Cassiopeia very much?" said Dr. Bryant, wishing to turn the current of her thoughts. "I think it very beautiful, particularly when it occupies its present position, and, as it were, offers to weary travelers so inviting a seat. Yet often I am strangely awed, in gazing on the group so enveloped in unfathomable mystery. Who may say when another of its jewels shall flicker and go out? And when may not our own world to other planets be a 'Lost Star?' How childish associations cling to one in after years. I never looked up at Cassiopeia, without recalling the time when my tutor gave me as a parsing lesson the first lines of the 'Task'—literally a task to me (mind I do not claim the last as original, for it is a plagiarism on somebody, I forget now who). My teacher first read the passage carefully over, explaining each idea intended to be conveyed, and at the conclusion turned to an assistant, and remarked that 'with

Cassiopeia for a model, he wondered chairs were not earlier constructed.' I wondered in silence what that hard word could signify? and at length summoned courage to ask an explanation. A few nights afterward, visiting at my father's, he took me out, pointed to the constellation, and gave the origin of the name, while, to my great joy, I discovered the resemblance to a chair. Ah! that hour is as fresh in my memory as though I stood but last night by his side and listened to his teachings."

"Yes, who will deny the magic influence of association? After all, Dr. Bryant, it is not the intrinsic beauty of an object that affords us such delight, but ofttimes the memory of the happy past, so blended with the beauty viewed as scarcely to be analyzed in the soothing emotions which steal into the heart. Such a night as this ever reminds me of the beautiful words of Willis, in his 'Contemplations;' and, like Alethe, I often ask, ' When shall I gather my wings, and, like a rushing thought, stretch onward, star by star, up into heaven?'"

A silence ensued for several moments, and then the cry of " Water!" " water!" fell refreshingly on the ears of the wearied travelers, and the neighboring stream was hailed as joyfully as was in olden time the well of Zem-Zem.

Soon the tents were pitched, and a bright crackling fire kindled. Florence, declaring she was too much fatigued for supper, threw herself on her pallet. Aunt Lizzy and Mrs. Carlton were busily unpacking some of their utensils, and Mary, closely wrapt up, stood by the blazing logs, thinking how cheerful i*s* ruddy light made every object seem, and wondering if, after all, the Ghebers were so much to blame. Mr. Carlton joined her; and after inquiring how she bore their very fatiguing ride, remarked that in a few more days their journeyings would be over.

"I shall almost regret its termination. This mode of traveling seems very pleasant to me, and you who are strong and well, must enjoy it much more."

Just then the sound of approaching hoofs caused her to look toward their wagon; and she perceived two men mounted, one in the act of descending, while Dr. Bryant advanced quickly to meet him.

Mr. Carlton left her. Silently she looked on, wondering who the strangers could possibly be, when the words fell with startling distinctness on her listening ear:

"Dudley Stewart! do my eyes deceive me?"

"Frank Bryant! is it possible I meet you here?"

The tones of the last speaker were too familiar to be mistaken. She trembled from head to foot as the past rose before her. Her first thought was of Florence.

"Oh, if he is married, this meeting will be terrible!" and her heart throbbed violently as the gentlemen approached her. Scarce conscious of her movements, she advanced to meet Dr. Bryant, whose arm was linked in that of the new comer. They met: the fire-light glowed on the face of both.

"Mr. Stewart!" and the wasted hand was extended.

"Mary Irving! or is this an illusion?" Tightly the hand was clasped.

"It is I—your old pupil, though so altered, I wonder not that you fail to recognize me." She lifted her eyes and met Dr. Bryant's gaze, deep and piercing, as though he were reading her inmost soul. Mr. Stewart looked long at the face turned toward him.

"Frank, you did not tell me she was with you! Oh, how changed—how wasted you are! But what means this black dress?" and his fingers clutched her mourning gown, while his deep tone faltered. Mary drew closer to his side, and murmured:

"Florry is well; but my uncle has been taken from us." Her head sunk on her bosom as she spoke.

"Where is Florence?" and he tightly clasped her hand between his own.

A shudder crept over Dr. Bryant, who had not heard their words, and he walked quickly away.

"Florry is in the tent. Mr. Stewart, we heard that you were married; can this be true?"

"No, no! Did your cousin credit the report?"

"Yes; and ere you make yourself known, let me in some degree prepare her for the meeting."

So saying, she sought Florence, and asked if she were sleeping.

"No, Mary; can I do any thing for you?" and she raised her head.

"Yes, Florry, come with me—I want to speak to you."

Her cousin accompanied her to the door, and standing so that the tent intervened between them and Mr. Stewart, Mary laid her hand on Florence's shoulder, and said:

"I have just learned, Florry, that Mr. Stewart is not married."

"Mary, Mary! why touch a chord which ever vibrates with the keenest agony? There is no happiness for me on earth—I have known that for long, and now I am striving to fix my thoughts, and all of hope that remains on heaven."

Mary linked her arm in Florence's, and gently drawing her forward, replied:

"God has not promised heaven as the price of every earthly joy and comfort. Can you not still hope for happiness?"

"Mary, I am parted forever from him whom I have loved so devotedly; yet I cease to repine. I know my lot, and I will pass through life alone, yes, alone, without a murmur."

"Not so, Florence—my own treasured Florence!"

She turned quickly, and was clasped to the heart of him she had sworn to love alone.

"Am I dreaming?" said Florence, gazing eagerly up into the noble face before her. He lifted his cap from his brow, and bent his head that the light might fall full upon it. A gleam of perfect joy irradiated her beautiful face, and, leaning her head on his shoulder, she whispered: "Forgive me—for I doubted you."

He bent, and sealed her pardon with a long kiss.

Mary stole away to Mrs. Carlton to impart the good news; Dr. Bryant had already communicated it. Warmly she sympathized with them in again meeting an old friend; but Mary heeded not her words, for her eyes were riveted on Frank's stern brow and slightly curling lip. A mist rose before her, and catching for support at the tent, she would have fallen, had not his strong arm encircled her; and soon she lay motionless in her tent. He stood and looked on her a moment, then knelt and clasped the cold hands. Mary had not swooned, though well-nigh insensible, and a low moan of anguish escaped her lips, colorless, and writhing with pain.

"Can I do nothing for you?"

"No, thank you; only do not tell Florry and Mr. Stewart I am ill. It would only damp the joy of their meeting."

He left her, and met the lovers as they sought the remainder of the party. He understood at a glance the position of affairs, and with the sad conviction that Mary loved Mr. Stewart, and loved him in vain, he strove to repress his emotion and appear as usual.

Florence withdrew her hand from Mr. Stewart's clasp, and, with a deep blush, passed Frank in order to reach the tent. He placed himself before it.

"Miss Hamilton, I can't allow any one to disturb your cousin; she is almost exhausted by our long ride, and I forbid all company, as she needs rest and quiet."

"I will not disturb her in the least, I assure you, Doctor." But he persisted, and she was forced to form one of the circle that now gathered round the fire.

Mr. Stewart, in answer to Dr. Bryant's inquiries, replied that he had long felt anxious to visit San Antonio, but had been detained at home by important business till within a few weeks, when he set out for Austin, and obtaining there a sort of guide and companion, was hastening on, hoping to reach the former place ere the arrival of the Mexican forces.

"Having heard," continued he, "that Mr. Hamilton's death had left his family somewhat unprotected, I felt particularly anxious on their account. Seeing your camp-fire, attracted us in this direction, and happy am I to meet so many old friends."

To Florence he had been far more explicit, detailing the causes which produced a most fortunate change in his circumstances, and his immediate determination to seek her in her Western home.

"You will return with us to Washington then, Stewart, as we possess the treasure you are in search of?"

"Yes, if none of the party offers any objection," replied he.

"I don't know that any feel disposed to act so ungratefully: suppose we inquire, however. Miss Hamilton, have you any objections to receiving as an escort and protector, this amiable cavalier, who has wandered so far from home to offer his services?"

"Frank, it is hardly fair to make her speak for the party; some may differ with her, on so important a point."

"You seem quite certain as to her sentiments on this subject. Upon my word, Miss Florence, if I were you, I should most assuredly take this occasion to teach him a little humility; for instance, just tell him it makes no difference with you—that it is perfectly immaterial."

"In following your advice, Doctor, the responsibility will be inevitably transferred to yourself; and I must thank you for so politely relieving me."

"I see no reason, Stewart, why you should not join our party, and lend your assistance toward enlivening the tedious hours yet in store for us; though only a few more days of travel remain, thank Heaven."

"One would suppose, from the fear of ennui which seems to cloud your future, that Mary and I had not succeeded so happily as we imagined, in our efforts to entertain you."

"Pardon me, Miss Florence, if I have failed duly to appreciate your kind efforts: though candor compels the avowal, that I was not aware any extraordinary exertion was made in my behalf."

"Really, Frank, I should say you have made considerable progress in raising yourself in your own estimation since last I heard you converse. Mrs. Carlton, I am afraid this climate is unfavorable for the growth of at least two of the cardinal virtues."

"Your insinuation is contemptible because utterly without grounds. Miss Florence, I appeal to you, as worthy the privilege of acting as umpire in this important discusion. Have you ever observed aught in my conduct indicating a want of humility?"

"Unfortunately, Doctor, should I return an answer in your favor, it would be at the expense of a virtue equally entitled to pre-eminence."

"To be very candid, Miss Hamilton, I must return thanks for her disinterested and very flattering decision."

Here the conversation was interrupted by a call to the evening meal, and gladly they obeyed the welcome summons.

Florence glancing round perceived the absence of her cousin, and inquired the cause.

"I dare say she is asleep, poor child," said Aunt Lizzy.

"She is trying to rest, Miss Hamilton, and I would not advise any interruption. She needs quiet, for she was sorely tried by this day's fatigue," observed Dr. Bryant.

"I am afraid so," replied Florence, an anxious look again settling on her face. "Oh, I wish on her account we could reach a place of rest and safety. I fear she has failed in strength since leaving San Antonio."

"How sadly changed she has become: had she not spoken in her old, familiar tones, I should not have known her. I earnestly hope there is nothing serious in her attack, and that she will soon regain her former bloom: it pains me to see her so altered," said Mr. Stewart.

"She can not possibly improve while subjected to the fatigues of this journey. I feared she was scarce able to endure it," answered Frank.

The conversation turned on more agreeable topics, and soon—by all but Frank, who could not forget her look of anguish—she was for a time forgotten.

Mary heard from her couch of suffering the cheerful blending of voices, though nothing distinct reached her ear; and as none approached to soothe her by affectionate inquiries, a sense of neglect stole over her. But too habitually accustomed to judge gently of others and forget herself, it passed quickly away. She knelt on her pallet, and clasping her thin hands, raised her heart to God, in the low, feeble tone of one well-nigh spent:

"My God, thou readest my heart? Thou knowest how, day by day, I have striven to love thee more and serve the better. Yet, oh, Father of mercies! my soul is tortured with unutterable agony! Oh! on the verge of the tomb, my heart still clings to earth and its joys. Look down in thy mercy upon me, and help me to fix my thoughts on heaven and thee. For long I have known the vanity of my hope, and the deceitfulness of human things: yet I could not tear away the pleasing image, and turn to thee alone for comfort. Oh, may peace be my portion the few days I have to live, and when death comes, be thou with me, my God, to comfort and take me soon to my home above."

She sank back in very weariness. "Oh, Frank, how could you so mistake me?—you whom I have loved so long, how could you believe I loved another?"

In the clear sunny light of morning, how cheerful all things looked; and to a heart at peace with God, nature seemed rejoicing. The deep blue vault arching illimitably above—the musical murmuring of the creek, as it rushed along its rocky bed—the mosquit, bent and glittering with its frosty mantle, blended with the blazing camp-fire and the busy hum of preparation for the day, stole pleasingly into the heart. All the party, save Mary, stood about the fire, warming their fingers and chatting on the various occurrences of their long journey. All paused to welcome the invalid, as she joined them with a slow, feeble step; yet she looked better than she had done since leaving her home. Restlessly she had tossed on her hard couch, and now the hectic flush mantled the thin cheek and brightened the deep blue eyes. The warm congratulations of her friends on her improved appearance brought a sad smile to her lip, and the expression of Dr. Bryant's countenance told her that he at least realized her danger. Never had Florence looked more beautiful, as the clear cold air brought the glow to her cheek, added to the effect of her mourning dress and the expression of quiet happiness, imparting an indescribable charm to her lovely features.

"As you now stand, Miss Florence, looking so

earnestly toward the east, you seem to me a perfect realization of Willis's Jeptha's Daughter:

> "'She stood before her father's gorgeous tent,
> To listen for his coming. Her loose hair
> Was resting on her shoulder, like a cloud
> Floating around a statue, and the wind
> Just swaying her light robe, revealed a shape
> Praxiteles might worship:
> Her countenance was radiant with love:
> She looked to die for it—a being whose
> Whole existence was the pouring out
> Of rich and deep affections.'"

As he looked upon her, these lines were uttered half unconsciously; and then turning to Mary, he gently asked if he might speak what was passing in his mind.

"Certainly, Frank—continue your quotation; the lines never seemed so beautiful before;" said Mr. Stewart glancing at Florence as he spoke.

"Doubtless not, Stewart, because never so applied. Miss Hamilton, your cousin looks more as did the Jewish maiden at close of evening:

> "'Her face was pale, but very beautiful; her lip
> Had a more delicate outline, and the tint
> Was deeper. But her countenance was like the
> Majesty of angels.'"

"Dr. Bryant, is it possible you so far forget yourself and previously expressed opinions, as to make quotations? I thought you a sworn foe to the practice."

"On ordinary occasions, I am; and you may rest

assured it is the last time I commit such an absurdity by a camp fire. I think you once asked me my objection—will you hear it now? When I was quite young, I one day read an anecdote of the celebrated Greek professor, Dr. Porson, which gave me a strong bias against quotations, particularly locating them, which necessarily follows. Porson was once traveling in a stage-coach, when a young Oxonian, fresh from college, was amusing some ladies with quite a variety of small talk, smong other things a quotation from Sophocles, as he said. A Greek quotation in a stage-coach roused Porson, who half slumbered in a quiet corner. 'Young gentleman,' said he, 'I think you indulged us, just now, with a quotation from Sophocles; I don't happen to remember it there.'—'Oh, sir,' rejoined the tyro, ' the quotation is word for word, and in Sophocles too.' The professor handed him a small edition of Sophocles, and requested him to point out the passage. After rummaging about for some time, he replied: ' Upon second thought the passage is in Euripides.' ' Then,' said Porson, handing him a similar edition of Euripides, ' perhaps you will be so kind as to find it for me in this little book.' Our young gentleman returned unsuccessfuly to the search, with the very pleasant cogitation of ' Curse me, if ever I quote Greek again in a stage-coach.' The tittering of the ladies increased his confusion, and desperate at last, he exclaimed—' Bless me, how dull I am; I remember now perfectly that the passage is in Æschylus.' The incorrigible professor dived again into his apparently bottomless pocket, and produced an edition of Æschylus; but the astounded Oxonian exclaimed, 'Stop the coach Halloa! coachman, let me out instantly; there is a fellow inside here that has got the whole Bodleian library in his pocket. Let me out, I say—it must be Porson or the devil!' Now previous to reading this anecote, I must confess to quite a *penchant* for quotations, but I assure you a full year elapsed ere I ventured on another; and for a long time the ghost of our gentleman appeared, spectre-like, before me, whenever I attempted one."

When the merriment subsided, Mr. Stewart asked if it was not of this same professor that a phrenologist remarked, on examining his skull, that " the most important question was, how the ideas found access to the brain—once inside, and there are very solid reasons to prevent their getting out again."

"Yes, the same. Craniologists admit, I believe, that his was the thickest skull ever examined; and it is related that when he could no longer articulate English, he spoke Greek with fluency."

In a few moments the camp was broken up, and they proceeded on their way. Mary cast a longing glance toward her horse, now mounted by one of the servants, and was taking her seat in the wagon, when Dr. Bryant said:

"Would you like to try your horse a little while this morning? If it proves too fatiguing, you can return to the wagon."

"I should like it very much, if I felt strong enough, but I could not sit upright so long. Doctor, will you be so kind as to ride my horse for me to-day, and let William drive?"

"Certainly, if you prefer it; but may I venture to ask your reason?"

"You have long been separated from your friend, and naturally wish to be with him. Do not, on my account, remain behind the party, as you are forced to do in driving the wagon, but join Florence and Mr. Stewart, who seem in such fine spirits this beautiful morning. I feel too weary and feeble to talk, and William will take good care of me."

He fixed his dark eyes mournfully on her face; she could not meet his gaze, and her head sunk upon her bosom.

"Believe me, Miss Irving, every other pleasure is second to that of watching over and being with you. If, in the proposed change, my feelings alone are to be consulted, allow me to remain with you."

"Thank you, Dr. Bryant, you are very kind to remember me so constantly; my only object was to promote your enjoyment of the day."

They rode for some distance in silence.

"This is my birth-day; and how little I fancied, on the last anniversary, that I should be so situated," said Dr. Bryant, as though speaking unconsciously.

"How one's feeling change with maturer years. I remember well that, in my childhood, the lapse of time seemed provokingly slow, and I wondered why, from year to year, it seemed so very long. The last three years of my life, though, somewhat checkered, have flown too quickly away. A month ago, I would willingly have recalled them, but they are lost in the ocean of eternity, only to be remembered now as a changing, feverish dream," Mary replied.

"Miss Irving, without the benign and elevating influence of Hope, that great actuating principle from the opening to the close of life, what a dreary blank our existence would prove. In childhood it gorgeously gilds the future; the tints fade as maturity gains that future, and then it gently brightens the evening of life, while memory flings her mantle of witchery over the past, recalling, in hours of sadness, all of joy to cheer the heart, and banishing forever the phantoms of terror—the seasons of gloom that once haunted us."

"Yes, how appropriately has the great bard of Time, termed Hope 'silver-tongued.' And then, its soothing accents are felt and acknowledged in the darkest hour of human trial. When about to sever every earthly tie—when on the eve of parting with every object rendered dear by nature and association —when the gloomy portals of the silent tomb open to receive us, then comes Hope to paint the joys of heaven. Our reunion with those we have loved and lost—perfect freedom from sin—the society of angels, and the spirits of the just made perfect; the presence of our Saviour, and an everlasting home in the bosom of our God."

A look of unutterable peace and joy settled on the face of Mary as she finished speaking and sank back, her hands clasped, and her eyes raised as though in communion with the spirits above.

Dr. Bryant's eyes rested with a sort of fascination on her countenance.

"You have this hope; yes, already your soul turns from earth and its vanities to the pure, unfailing fount of heavenly joy. Oh! that I, like you, could soon find peace and perfect happiness! I have striven against the bitter feelings which of late have crept into my heart; still, despite my efforts, they gather rapidly about me. I look forward, and feel sick at heart. Turbid are all the streams of earthly pleasures, and fully now I realize those lines, which once seemed the essence of misanthropy—

> 'I thought upon this hollow world,
> And all its hollow crew.'

For a time I found delight in intellectual pursuits, but soon wearied of what failed to bring real comfort in hours of trial."

"You need some employment to draw forth every faculty: in a life of active benevolence and usefulness, this will be supplied. Do not give vent to feelings of satiety or ennui; your future should be bright —no dangers threaten, and many and important duties await you in life. God has so constituted us, that happiness alone springs from the faithful discharge of these. Every earthly resource fails to bring contentment, unless accompained by an active, trusting fatih in God, and hope of blessedness in heaven. Wealth, beauty, genius are as naught; and fame, that hollow, gilded bauble, brings not the promised delight, and an aching void remains in the embittered heart. One of our most talented authors, now seated on the pinnacle of fame, assures us that

> 'The Sea of Ambition is tempest tost,
> And your hopes may vanish like foam.'
> * * * * *
> 'The Sun of Fame but gilds the name,
> The heart ne'er felt its ray.'

Pardon me if I have ventured too far, or wounded your feelings: it was not my intention, and I have spoken half unconsciously."

"Thank you, Miss Irving, for your kind words of comfort and advice. Fear not that ambition will lure me; I know its hollow, bitter wages, and can not be deceived. Yet there is a lonely feeling in my heart which I can not dispel at will. Still my plans for the future are sufficiently active to interest me; and I doubt not that a year hence I shall feel quite differently. If I could always have your counsel and sympathy, I should fear nothing."

"In seasons of trial—in the hours of gloom and despondency—appeal to your sister for comfort. Oh! she is far more capable of advising and cheering than I, who only echo her sentiments." Mary pressed her hand to her side, and leaning back, closed her eyes, as if longing for rest.

"I have drawn you on to converse more than was proper—forgive my thoughtlessness; and, if it would not be impossible, sleep, and be at rest." He carefully arranged her shawls, and as she lay a long while with closed eyes, he thought her sleeping, but turning, after a time, was surprised to perceive her gazing earnestly out on the beautiful country through which they now rode.

CHAPTER XVI.

> "Alas! how light a cause may move
> Dissensions between hearts that love!
> Hearts that the world in vain had tried,
> And sorrow but more closely tied;
> That stood the storm when waves were rough
> Yet in a sunny hour, fall off,
> Like ships that have gone down at sea,
> When heaven was al' tranquillity!"
>   —*Moore.*

PEACE and quiet and rest for you at last!" cried Dr. Bryant, as they drove into the village of Washington, and, by dint of much trouble and exertion, procured a small and comfortless house. But a bright fire soon blazed in the broad, deep, old-fashioned chimney—the windows and doors closed—their small stock of furniture and provisions unpacked, and a couch prepared for Mary, now far too feeble to sit up. The members of the safe and happy party gathered about the hearth, and discussed hopefully their future prospects. Dr. Bryant raised his eyes to the somewhat insecure roof,

through which the light of day occasionally stole in
and exclaimed:

'And doth a roof above me close.

"Not such a one as greeted Mazeppa on regaining his senses, Frank; rather insecure, 'tis true, yet somewhat better than the canvas covering for which we have been so grateful of late."

Dr. Bryant leaned his elbow on the mantle-piece, and fell into a fit of musing, not unusual to him since leaving San Antonio. The servant disturbed his reverie by requesting room for her cooking utensils. He raised his head as she spoke, and then, as if utterly unconscious, dropped it again, without reply.

"A segar for your thoughts, Bryant!" said Mr. Stewart, and linking his arm in that of his friend they turned away.

Florence approached her cousin, and bending over the wasted form, asked if she were not already better.

Mary lifted her arms to her cousin's neck, and for a moment strove to press her to her heart, but strength had failed rapidly of late, and they sank wearily by her side. Florence sat down and took both hands between hers.

"Tell me, dear, if you are in pain?"

"No, Florry, I do not suffer much now; I am at present free from all pain. I have not had an opportunity of talking with you for some time. Florry, tell me, are you very happy!"

"Yes, Mary, I am very happy—happier than I

ever was before; and far more so than I deserve. Oh! Mary, how miserable I have been; and it is by contrast that the transition is so delightful. I doubted the goodness and mercy of God, and, in the bitterness of my heart, I asked why I had been created for so much suffering. Oh, Mary! my pure-hearted, angel cousin, how much of my present happiness I owe to you. Suppose you had suffered me to wander on in a maze of darkness. At this moment I should have been a desolate, deluded, miserable nun; clinging to a religion which, instead of Bible truths, filled the anxious, aching heart with monkish legends of unattested miracles, and in place of the pure worship of God, gives us mummeries nearer akin to pagan rites! I thank God that I am released from my thralldom. I see now the tissue of falsehood so plausible in which all things were wrapped. Blackness and deceit in the garb of truth and purity! And it is horrible to think that he who so led me astray claims to be my brother! Mary, Mary, how can I tell Mr. Stewart this?—tell him that I have wondered from the true faith—that I have knelt in confession to him who cursed our common father! He will despise me for my weakness; for only yesterday he said he first loved me for my clear insight into right and wrong, and my scorn of deceit and hypocrisy! Yet I deceived you; at least, tacitly—you who have ever loved me so truly, you who have saved me at last, and pointed out the road to heaven. Mary forgive me! I never asked pardon of any on earth before, but I wronged you, good and gentle though you always were. Forgive me, oh, my cousin!"

Mary clasped Florence's hands in hers, and though too feeble to speak very audibly, replied:

"Florry, think not of the past; it has been very painful to us both, yet I thank God that you are right at last. You know how I love you: I would give every treasure of earth to contribute to your happiness; and now that you are so blest, listen to my counsel. Florry, there is a cloud no bigger than a man's hand resting low on the horizon of your happiness—be warned in time. You know Mr. Stewart's firm, unwavering principles of Protestantism; you know, too, the aversion with which he regards the priests of Rome; it may be a hard task now, but it will be tenfold more difficult a year hence. Go to him at once, tell him you were misguided and deceived, and reveal every circumstance connected with that unhappy period. He will love you more for your candor. Florry, you turn pale, as though unequal to the task. Oh, my cousin, you prize his love more than truth; but the time will come when he will prize truth more than your love! Florry, let me beg you tell him all, and at once." She sank back, as if exhausted by her effort in speaking so long, yet firmly retained Florence's hand.

"Mary, if I do this, it is at the risk of losing his esteem, which I prize even more than his love. And after all, *I* cannot see that truth or duty requires this humiliating confession. Should he ever question me, I should scorn to deceive him, and at once should tell him all. But he does not suspect it, and *I*, being no longer in danger or blinded, need not reveal the past."

Mournfully Mary regarded her beautiful cousin.

"Florry, if you conceal nothing now, he will esteem you more than ever for hazarding his love in the cause of truth. If, in after years, he discovers the past, he will tell you that, silently at least, you deceived him, and reproach you with want of candor and firmness. Oh! there is a fearful risk to run; he will never place confidence in you again—be warned in time."

The entrance of Aunt Lizzy and Mrs. Carlton prevented further conversation, and unclasping Mary's fingers, Florence disengaged her hand and left the room.

Two days passed in furnishing and arranging their new home, and Mary saw but little of her cousin. As evening closed in again, the invalid watched from her couch the countenance of Mr. Stewart, as he sat earnestly conversing with her aunt. Florence and Mr. and Mrs. Carleton were out making some necessary purchases, and Dr. Bryant had been absent on business of his own since morning."

"Florence is too young to marry, or even dream of it, at present, Mr. Stewart; and besides, if I must be candid, I have always entertained different views for her."

"Pardon me, but I believe I scarcely comprehend your meaning. You speak of other views for her; may I venture to ask the nature of these?"

"I have never expected her to marry at all, Mr. Stewart."

"And why not, pray? What can you urge in favor of your wishes?"

"I had her own words to that effect, scarce a month ago."

A proud, happy smile played round his lips, and he replied: "She may have thought so then, but I think her views have changed."

"But for Mary, she would have been the same:" and a bitter look passed over her wrinkled face.

"Excuse me, if I ask an explanation of your enigmatical language; there is some hidden meaning, I well know."

"Mr. Stewart, your mother and I are old friends and I wish you well; but all good Catholics love their church above every earthly thing. I should like to see Florence happy, but her eternal good should first be secured; you are a Protestant, and bitterly opposed to our Holy Church, and I cannot consent to see her marry a heretic, for such you are: she is too far astray already."

"If your niece were herself a Papist, your reason would indeed be a cogent one; but, under existing circumstances, I am puzzled to understand you."

"Were it not for Mary's influence, Florence would even now rest in the bosom of our Holy Church. She has done her cousin a grievous wrong; may God and the Blessed Virgin forgive her!"

Mary groaned in spirit, as she marked the stern glance of his eagle eye, and feebly raising herself, she said: "Mr. Stewart, will you take this seat beside the sofa? I wish to speak with you."

Aunt Lizzy left the room hurriedly, as though she had already heard too much, and silently he complied with Mary's request.

"You are pained and perplexed at what my aunt has just said; allow me to explain what may seem a great mystery. You are not aware that my uncle died a Papist. Weakened in body and mind by disease, he was sought and influenced in secret, when I little dreamed of such a change. On his deathbed he embraced the Romish faith, and, as I have since learned, exacted from Florry a promise to abide by the advice of his priest, in spiritual as well as temporal matters. He expired in the act of taking the sacrament, and our desolation of heart can be better imagined than described—left so utterly alone and unprotected, far from our relatives and the friends of our youth. I now marked a change in Florry, though at a loss to account for it. An influence, secret as that exerted on her lost parent, was likewise successful, and, to my grief and astonishment, I found that she too had embraced papacy."

The door opened and Florence entered. She started on seeing her lover, but advanced to them much as usual. He raised his head, and cold and stern was the glance he bent on her beautiful face. She stood beside him, and rising, he placed a chair for her in perfect silence. Mary's heart ached, as she noted the marble paleness which overspread her cousin's cheek. Mr. Stewart folded his arms across his chest, and said in a low, stern, yet mournful tone:

"Florence, I could not have believed that you would have deceived me, as you have silently done."

Mournfully Florence looked for a moment on Mary's face, yet there was no reproach in her glance; it seemed but to say—" You have wakened me from my dream of happiness."

She lifted proudly her head, and fixed her dark eyes full on her lover.

"Explain yourself, Mr. Stewart; I have a right to know with what I am charged, though I almost scorn to refute that of deceit."

"Not a week since, Florence, you heard me avow my dislike of the tenets and practices of the Romish Church. I said then, as now, that no strong-minded, intelligent woman of the present age could consult the page of history and then say that she conscientiously believed its doctrines to be pure and scriptural, or its practices in accordance with the teachings of our Saviour. You tacitly concurred in my opinions. Florence, did you tell me you had once held those doctrines in reverence? Nay, that even now you lean to papacy?" Stern was his tone, and cold and slightly contemptuous his glance.

A bitter, scornful smile wreathed the lips of his betrothed. "I acknowledge neither the authority of questioning, nor allow the privilege of any on earth to impugn my motives or my actions. Had I felt it incumbent on me to acquaint you with every circumstance of my past life, I should undoubtedly have done so, when you offered me your hand. I felt no obligation to that effect, and consequently consulted my own inclinations. If, for a moment, you had doubted me, or asked an explanation of the past, I should have scorned to dissemble with you; and now that the subject is broached you shall have the particulars, which, I assure you, have kept well, though, as you suppose, sometime withheld. I have been a member of the Church of Rome: I have prayed to saints and the Virgin, counted beads and used holy water, and have knelt in confession to a priest of papal Rome. I did all this, thinking, for a time, my salvation dependent on it. You know all now."

Mr. Stewart regarded her sadly as she uttered these words, and his stern tone softened as he noticed her bloodless cheek and quivering lip.

"Florence, it is not your former belief or practice that give me this pain, and sadden our future. If you were at this moment a professor of the Romish faith, I would still cherish and trust you; I should strive to convince you of your error—to point out the fallacy of your hopes. When I recall the circumstances by which you were surrounded, and the influencs exerted, I scarcely wonder that, for a time, you lent your credence and support. But, Florence, full well you know that this is not what pains me. It is the consciousness that you have kept me in ignorance of what your own heart told you would show your momentary weakness, and led me to suppose you entertained a belief at variance with your practice. You have feared my displeasure more than the disregard of truth and candor. Florence, Florence! knowing how well I loved you, and what implicit confidence I reposed in you, how could you do this?"

"Again, Mr. Stewart, I repeat that I perceive no culpability in my conduct. Had I felt it my duty, your love or indifference would not have weighed an atom in my decision to act according to my sense of right and wrong."

He turned from her, and paced to and fro before the fire. Florence would have left the room, but Mary clasped her dress, and detained her.

"Mr. Stewart, you have been too harsh and hasty in your decision, and too severe in your remarks. Florry has not forfeited your love, though she acted imprudently. Ask your own heart whether you would be willing to expose to her eye your every foible and weakness. For you, like all God's creatures, have faults of our own. Is there nothing you have left untold relative to your past? Oh! if you knew how deep and unutterable has been her love, even when she never again expected to meet you, you would forget this momentary weakness—a fault committed from the very intensity of her love, and fear lest she should sink in your estimation."

"Mary, if she had said, Dudley, I have not always felt as now, and my mind was darkened for a time, I should have loved her, if possible, more than before, for her noble candor. My own heart would have told me, This is one in whom you may eternally trust, for she risked the forfeiture of your love in order that truth might be unsullied How can I confide in one who values the esteem of man more than the approval of her own conscience? You have said her love was a palliation. No, you are wrong; it is an aggravation of her fault. She should have loved me too well to suffer me to discover by chance what should have been disclosed in confidence. Mary, her love is not greater than mine. None know how I have cherished her memory— how I have kept her loved image in my heart during our long separation. I would give every earthly joy or possession to retain her affection, for it is dearer to me than everything beside, save truth, candor and honesty. I have nothing to conceal from her. I would willingly bare my secret soul to her scrutiny. There is nothing I should wish to keep back, unless it be the pain of this hour."

He paused by her side, and looked tenderly on the pale, yet lovely face of Florence.

"Mr. Stewart, shall one fault forever destroy your confidence in Florry, when she has declared that had she thought it incumbent on her to speak of these things—if she had felt as you do, she asserts that nothing could have prevented her revealing every circumstance."

"Mary, I fear her code of morality is somewhat too lax; and the fact that she acknowledges no fault is far more painful than any other circumstance."

"Mary, I have omitted one thing which I wish

him to know. I neglected to inform you, that the priest to whom I confessed is my half-brother! I have now told you all; and thinking as you do, it is better that in future we forget the past and be as strangers to each other. That I have loved you fervently, I can never forget—neither your assertion that I am unworthy of your confidence."

She disengaged her dress from Mary's clasp, and turned toward the door. Mr. Stewart caught her hand, and firmly held it. She struggled not to release herself, but lifted her dark eyes to his, and calmly met his earnest glance.

" Florence!"

There was a mournful tenderness in the deep tone. Her lip quivered, still her eyes fell not beneath his, piercing as an eagle's.

" Mr. Stewart, you have wronged her; you have been too severe." And Mary clasped his hand tightly, and looked up appealingly. He withdrew his hand.

" Florence, this is a bitter, bitter hour to me. Yet I may have judged too harshly: we will forget the past, and, in future, let no such cloud come between us."

" Not so, Mr. Stewart: if I am unworthy, how can you expect confidence from me ? Think you I will change the code which you just now pronounced too lax? Oh! you know not what you have done. It is no light thing to tell a woman of my nature she is unworthy of the love she prized above every earthly thing!" Her voice, despite her efforts, faltered.

" Florence, I have been too severe in my language, and you too proud and haughty. Full well we know that without the love of each other life would be joyless to both. Ours is not a common love; and again I say, let us forget the past, while, in future, need I ask you to keep nothing from me ?"

He drew her to him as he spoke, and passing his arm round her, pressed her to his heart. A long time Florence hid her head on his shoulder, as if struggling with her emotion, and then a heavy sob relieved her troubled heart. Closer he clasped her to him, and, laying his cheek on hers, murmured:

" My own darling Florence, forgive me, if I misjudged you; tell me that you will not remember my words—that this hour shall be to us as a painful dream."

She withdrew from his embrace, and, lifted her head, replied:

" I was wrong to doubt your love, or believe that you would think long of my weakness; but I am innocent of the charge of dissimulation, and never let us recur to the past."

She held out her hand, and clasping it in his, Mr. Stewart led her away.

An hour later Mary lay with closed eyes, too weary, from over excitement, even to look about her. All had left the room, and a dim light from the hearth just faintly lighted the large, comfortless apartment. With noiseless step Dr. Bryant entered, and seating himself in the vacant chair, near Mary's sofa, bent forward that he might look on the wan face of the sufferer. His heart ached as he noted the painful alteration of the last week, and gently and softly he took one of the thin white hands between his own. It was cold and damp, and, while he pressed it, the dark blue eyes rested earnestly on his face.

"I hoped you were sleeping, did I wake you?" and he laid the hand back, as she strove to withdraw it.

"No, I have not slept since morning."

"Oh! I am troubled at your constant suffering; is there any thing I can do for you?"

"No, thank you, Doctor, I wish nothing."

"All my arrangements are completed, and tomorrow I return to your home. Can I deliver any message, or execute any commission?"

For a moment Mary closed her eyes, then replied in a low voice:

"If you should see Inez, tell her to remember my gift at parting, and thank her, in my name, for her many, many kindnesses." She paused, as if gathering courage to say something more.

"And tell her, too, that ere many hours I shall be at rest. Tell her I have no fear, nay more, that I have great hope, and that heaven is opening for me. Let her prepare to join me, where there is no sorrow nor parting."

There was a silence, as if they were communing with their own hearts.

"You go to-morrow, Dr. Bryant? Then you will not stay to see me die? I am failing fast, and when you return, I shall have gone to that bourne whence no traveler comes back to tell the tale. Let me thank you now, for your unvarying kindness; many have been your services, and a brother's care has ever followed me. Thank you! I appreciate your kindness, and earnest and heartfelt is my prayer that you may be very happy and blest on earth; and when you, too, come to die, may your end be like mine—free from all fear, and may hope and joy attend your last moments!"

Her breathing grew short, and large drops stood on her pure, beautiful brow.

He had bent his head upon his bosom while she spoke, but now he raised it, and, taking her hand, clasped it warmly.

"Mary, Mary, if you knew what torture you inflicted, you would spare me this!"

It was the first time he had called her Mary, and her pale lip quivered.

"Forgive me, if I cause you pain!"

Bending forward, he continued, in a tone of touching sadness—" I had determined, Mary, to keep my grief locked in my own heart, and never to let words of love pass my lips. But the thought of parting with you forever is more than I can bear. Oh! Mary, have you not seen for weeks and months how I have loved you? Long ago, when first we met, a deep, unutterable love stole into my heart. I fancied for a time that you returned it, till the evening we met at my sister's, and you spoke with such indifference of leaving me behind. I saw then I had flattered myself falsely; that you entertained none save friendly feelings toward me. Still I thought in time you might learn to regard me with warmer sentiments. So I hoped on till the evening of our last ride, when your agitation led me to suppose you loved another. I saw you meet Mr. Stewart, and was confirmed in my supposition. I gave up all hope of ever winning your affection in return. Now I see my error in believing for a moment that you felt otherwise to him than as a brother, as the betrothed of your cousin. I know that you have never loved him, and pardon my error. When I sought you just now, it was to say good-by, and in absence and varied and exciting pursuits to shut out from my heart the memory of my hopes and fears. Mary, your words fill me with inexpressible anguish! Oh, you can not know how blank and dreary earth will seem when you are gone! I shall have no hope, no incitement, no joy!"

As she listened to this confession, which a month before would have brought the glow to her cheek and sparkle to her eye, she felt that it came too late; still a perfect joy stole into her heart. She turned her face toward him, and gently said:

"I am dying; and, feeling as I do, that few hours are allotted me, I shall not hesitate to speak freely and candidly. Some might think me deviating from the delicacy of my sex; but, under the circumstances, I feel that I am not. I have loved you long, and to know that my love is returned, is a source of deep and unutterable joy to me. You were indeed wrong to suppose I ever regarded Mr. Stewart otherwise than as Florry's future husband. I have never loved but one."

"Mary, can it be possible that you have loved me, when I fancied, of late, that indifference, and even dislike, nestled in your heart? We shall yet be happy! I thank God that we shall be so blest!" And he pressed the thin hand to his lips.

"Do not deceive yourself. Your confession has come too late. I can never be yours, for the hand of death is already laid upon me, and my spirit will wing its way, ere long, home to God. Now that we understand each other, and while I yet live, let us be as calm, as happy as the circumstances allow. It may seem hard that I should be taken when the future appears so bright, but I do not repine, neither must you. God, ever good and merciful, sees that it is best I should go, and we will not embitter the few hours left us by vain regrets." Too feeble to speak more, she closed her eyes, while her breathing grew painfully short.

Dr. Bryant bent forward, and gently lifting her head, supported her with his strong arm, and stroked off from her beautiful brow the clustering hair. A long time she lay motionless, with closed eyes, and bending his head, he pressed a long kiss on the delicately-chiseled lips.

"O God! spare me my gentle angel, Mary," he murmured, as looking on the wan, yet lovely face, he felt that to yield her up was more than he could bear.

At this moment Mrs. Carlton entered: he held out his hand, and drawing her to his side, said, in a deep, tender tone.

"She is mine now, sister; thank God, that at last I have won her and pray with me that she may be spared to us both."

Fervently she pressed his hand, and a tear rolled down and dropped upon it, as she bent down to kiss the sufferer. Gently he put her back.

"She is wearied, and just fallen asleep; do not wake her."

He carefully depressed his arm that she might rest more easily. Mrs. Carlton seated herself beside her brother, and whispered:

"You will not go to-morrow, Frank?"

"No, no; I will not leave her a moment. Ellen, does she seem very much thinner since leaving home? I know she is very pale."

"Yes, Frank; she is fearfully changed within the last week."

"Oh, Ellen! if she should be taken from me;" and closer he drew his arm, as though fearing some unseen danger.

"We must look to Heaven for her restoration, and God is good," answered his sister, turning away to conceal her tears.

CHAPTER XXVIII.

> "Ah! whence yon glare
> That fires the arch of heaven?—that dark red smoke
> Blotting the silver moon? . . .
> Hark to that roar, whose swift and deafening peals,
> In countless echoes, through the mountains ring,
> Startling pale midnight on her starry throne.
> * * * * * *
> Loud and more loud, the discord grows,
> Till pale Death shuts the scene,
> And o'er the conqueror and the conquered draws
> His cold and bloody shroud."
> —*Shelley*.

THE 6th of March rose dark and lowering, and all nature wore an aspect meet for the horrors which that day chronicled in the page of history. Toward noon the dense leaden cloud floated off, as though the uncertainty which vailed the future had suddenly been lifted—the crisis had come. Santa Anna and his blood-thirsty horde, rendered more savage by the recollection of the 11th December, poured out the vial of their wrath on the doomed town. Oh! San Antonio, thou art too beautiful for strife and discord to mar thy quiet loveliness. Yet the fiery breath of desolating war swept rudely o'er thee, and, alas! thou wast sorely scathed.

A second time the ill-fated fortress was fiercely charged. Long it withstood the terrible shock, and the overwhelming thousands that so madly pressed its gray, mouldering walls. The sun went down as it were in a sea of blood, its lurid light, gleaming ominously on the pale, damp brows of the doomed garrison. Black clouds rolled up and vailed the heavens in gloom. Night closed prematurely in with fitful gusts, mingling the moans and strife of nature with the roar of artillery. Still the fury of the onset abated not: the Alamo shook to its firm basis. Despairingly the noble band raised their eyes to the blackened sky. "God help us!" A howling blast swept by, lost in the deep muttering of the cannonade. Then a deep voice rung clearly out, high above the surrounding din: "Comrades, we are lost! let us die like brave men!"

The shriek of departing hope was echoed back by the sullen groan of despair. Travis fell, fighting at the entrance. As the hero sank upon the gory floor, there was a pause; friend and foe gazed upon the noble form! His spirit sprang up to meet his God.

"On, comrades! Travis has fallen! dearly will we die!"

One hundred and fifty brave hearts poured out their life-blood by his motionless form, struck down like sheep in the slaughter-pen. But seven remained: in despair they gaze on the ruin around, reeling from exhaustion and slipping in gore. There was borne on the midnight air a faint, feeble cry: "Quarter! quarter!" Alas! brave hearts, the appeal was lost, for an incarnate demon led the thirsty band. With a fiendish yell it was answered back,

"No quarter!" and ye seven were stretched beside yon fearless noble Travis.

Not a living Texan remained. The stiffening forms, grim in death, returned not even a groan to the wild shout of triumph that rung so mockingly through the deserted chambers of the slaughter-house. Victory declared for the wily tyrant—the black-hearted Santa Anna. Complete was the desolation which reigned around: there was none to oppose—no not one; and the Alamo was his again! Oh, Death! thou art insatiate! Hundreds had yielded to thy call, and followed the beckoning of thy relentless hand: and still another must swell thy spectre host, and join the shadowy band of the Spirit World!

For three days Don Garcia lay motionless on his couch of pain; even utterance was denied him, for paralysis had stretched forth her numb, stiffening finger, and touched him, even while he stood in the busy haunts of men. All day the din of battle had sounded in his ear; Inez from time to time stole from his side, and looked out toward the fortress, dimly seen through the sulphurous cloud of smoke and the blaze of artillery.

In the silent watches of the night, the shout of "Victory!" was borne on by the blast. "My father, the Alamo is taken—Santa Anna has conquered!" He struggled fearfully, a gurgling sound alone passed his lips, and he fell back lifeless on his pillow.

Calmly the girl bent down and closed the eyes, covered decently the convulsed features, and then, shrouding her face with the mantilla, stept forth for assistance. The next day saw the Don borne to his last resting-place. In accordance with the custom of the nation, no female followed the bier. It was borne by two men, and followed by some dozen children, and perhaps as many aged Mexicans, while just in advance strode the Padre, repeating the Latin service for the dead, and attended by four boys—two bearing censers, one a cross, and the other holy water. With indecent haste they pressed forward, passing through the church, and resting the bier for a moment on the altar, while an Ave Maria was repeated. At a sign from the Padre, the procession moved on to the churchyard, and, without further ceremony, the body was deposited in consecrated ground. Holy water was sprinkled profusedly around, and then all departed, leaving him to sleep undisturbed the last dreamless sleep.

Night found Inez sitting alone by her dreary, deserted hearth. Father, mother, sister, cousin, all had passed on before her; and the last of her house, she mused in her lonely home. A faint fire flickering on the hearth just revealed the form and face of the Mexican maiden. Her mantilla lay on the floor beside her, the black hair, thick and straight, hung to the waist, her brilliant, piercing eyes were bent vacantly on the fire, her dark cheek perfectly colorless as clay.

"Who is there to care for Inez now? Who will smoothe my pillow, and close my eyes, and lay me to rest?"

Her desolation of heart conquered; her head sunk upon her bosom, and a deep, bitter groan burst from her lips. Slowly she rocked herself to and fro in the loneliness of her spirit.

She had not loved her father warmly; there was little congeniality between them, and her hasty rejection of Mañuel's suit mutually embittered their intercourse. For Nevarro, a sort of sisterly feeling was entertained, no warmer affection. Yet she could love intensely. A little sister had waked her tenderness—her heart clung to the gentle child, so unlike herself. She sickened, and in a day went down to the tomb: bitter was the grief of Inez, who felt little for her mother, and soon she too took her place in the churchyard. Dr. Bryant came, and again Inez loved—again she was disappointed; and now she sat alone in the wide world, without one remaining tie to bind the future.

The hour of bitterness had come. She looked upon that dreary future and her utter desolation, and no gleam of hope stole to her darkened soul. An almost vacant expression settled on the dark countenance of the once beautiful maiden. Softly the door was pushed ajar, and the form of the Padre stood within. By instinct she seemed aware of his entrance, for raising her bowed head, the black sparkling eyes flashed, and the broad brow wrinkled into a frown dark as night. He approached her and they stood face to face upon the hearth.

"What do you do here, in the house of death, Mio Padre?"

"Inez, my queen of beauty, I have come to take the prize for which I toiled. There are none now between us, no, not one. You need not draw back so proudly."

A bitter, contemptuous laugh rung out on the night air, and Inez folded her arms upon her bosom.

"Truly, Padre, we are well mated! You have opposed me, and I thwarted you! I am your equal: think you to intimidate me with threats? You should know better!"

"Inez, listen! I leave this place before many days. My work is finished here; there are none to oppose, and I go elsewhere. To Mexico first, and then to Italy. You must go with me, my proud beauty! I cannot leave you here!"

Again Inez laughed her mocking laugh. "Go with you, Mio Padre! No, no; I must decline the honor. The hour of settlement has come! Alphonso Mazzolin, for long you have plotted my destruction; and one by one removed every obstacle in your way, and smoothed my path to ruin! I have known this—silently I have watched you manoeuvre. You counseled Mañuel; you flattered him, encouraged his hasty course and overbearing manner, and caused the rupture between us. You knew my nature, and foresaw the result. You thought to secure me within the walls of yonder gloomy convent, and hoped that in time my broad lands would bless and enrich your holy church! But, Padre, I did not fancy the home prepared for me in San Jose. I promised to comply with my father's wish, and fulfill the engagement, much to your surprise and chagrin. Padre, I would have married Mañuel, sooner than second your plans. I, too, foresaw the tempest that even now howls over us. It was my only hope, and I said, who may predict the chances of war? The Americans may yet number the most here, and then your power will be at an end. Seemingly I was passive, but you are thwarted. We stand face to face, and I scorn you, incarnate devil as you are. How dared you do as you have done? Mine eyes are opened—you can no longer deceive me with your lying legends and the marvellous traditions of your country. I tell you, I hate you with an everlasting hate. You have led me far from God, if there be a God, and may my curse follow you, even to your grave!"

Fiercely the glowing face was bent upon him. Hate, scorn, bitterness of heart, and utter desolation mingled strangely in the withering glance. The Padre seized her arm and hoarsely exclaimed:

"We know each other now; no matter, you cannot escape me; if force be necessary to take you hence, I can command it at any moment. You know full well my word is law; resist not, nor further rouse me—there is no help for you save in submission. I will not leave you."

"Ere I follow you hence, yonder river shall close over my body. I tell you now I will not accompany you."

He stepped to the door and whistled faintly. The

next moment a black-browed soldier stood before them.

"Herrara, she has broken her promise—she refuses to enter a convent, and she defies me, and scorns our holy church. I somewhat expected this; and I charge you now, suffer her not to pass the threshold of her own room; guard well the door, there is no window. See you, Inez, you can not escape me?"

He whispered in the intruder's ear, and, promising to come again the ensuing day, left the house, carefully closing the door after him. Lighting his cigarrita, Herrara requested Inez to seek her own apartment, that he might secure the door outside, and then return to the fire. Without a word she ascended the stairs to her own room. A chain was passed about the door, and then the retreating steps of the soldier died away.

What should she do? Inez sat down to collect her thoughts, and looked round the apartment. The walls were of solid rock, and in one corner was a small grating of four iron bars, which admitted light and air, but precluded all hope of escape in that quarter. The door was secured, and no means of egress presented itself. Her eye rested on her lamp, and a smile lit up the dark countenance of the prisoner. She threw herself on her bed; slowly the hours rolled—midnight came at last. She rose and listened—no stir, no sound of life reached her; she glanced at her lamp, now dim—the light was waning, and softly stepping across the room, she drew from a basket several bundles of papers. These she tore in pieces, and placing them beside the door, drew the lamp near. Inez carefully twisted up her long black hair, and placed on her head a broad sombrero, which the Don had worn of late; then taking his Mexican blanket, she slipped her head through the opening, and suffered it to fall to her feet. Something seemed forgotten, and after some little search she found a small cotton bag, into which she dropped a polonce, then secured it beneath the blanket. Queerly enough she looked, thus accoutred; but apparently the oddity of her appearance never once crossed her mind, for, stepping across the floor, she held the pieces of paper over the lamp till ignited, then quickly thrust them one by one between the small crack or chink in the centre of the door. It was of wood, old and dry, and caught like tinder. She watched it burn; the door was narrow, and the devouring element soon consumed all save the top and bottom pieces which extended across. These quivered as their support crumbled beneath them, and soon would fall with a crash. She watched her time, and gathering dress and blanket closely about her, sprang through, and though almost suffocated with smoke, hurried down to a small door at the rear of the house. She stood without and listened; Inez fancied she heard the crackling of the fire, yet there was no time to lose. Just before her sat a large stone vessel containing the soaking corn for the morning tortillos; drawing forth her bag she filled it with the swollen grain, and hastened on to where a small black horse was lassoed, having his hay scattered on the ground beside him. It was but the work of a moment to throw on and fasten her father's saddle, which hung on a neighboring tree, and loosing the hair lariat, she patted the pony she had often ridden on St. ——'s day, and sprang into the seat. Slowly she passed through the narrow yard and entered the street; pausing, she glanced up at her window, and perceived through the grating the blaze and smoke now filling the vacant room. Distinctly the clank of the chain fell on her ear, and turning into an alley she galloped away.

Inez knew it would be impossible to pass over the bridge and down the Alameda without detection, for seven hundred Mexican troops were stationed on the outskirts of the town; and, with the celerity of thought, she directed her way in the opposite direction, toward a shallow portion of the river, occasionally used as a ford. Happily the distance was short; and urging her somewhat unwilling horse, she plunged in. The moon rose full and bright as she reached the opposite bank; and pausing a moment, she looked back upon the sleeping town. No sound of life fell on her ear; and avoiding the beaten track, she turned her horse out on the grass, and hastened on toward the east, directing her course so as to pass beyond the Powder-House, which was dimly seen in the distance. At a quick canter it was soon passed, and she pressed on to the Salado, some three miles distant. Full well she knew she would be sought for when morning dawned; and with such speed she almost flew on, that sunrise found her many miles from her home. Inez was fearless, or she would never have dared to undertake what lay before her Alone, unprotected, in the guise of a man, without possessing his ordinary means of defence, there was much to risk; for Indian depredations were frequent and she must traverse a wide waste of almost interminable length ere reaching any settlement.

When the sunbeams played joyously about her Inez stopped to rest, and eating a few grains of her treasured corn, she allowed her horse to graze a short time along the margin of a stream, where the grass was tender and abundant; and then remounting, rode on somewhat more leisurely than she had previously done.

CHAPTER XXIX.

"To die, is landing on some silent shore,
Where billows never beat nor tempests roar!"
—Garth.

SINCE morning, Mary had lain in the deep, dreamless sleep of exhaustion: and now the leafless boughs, which waved to and fro before her window, threw long shadows aftwart the wall and across the deserted yard. Evening was creeping slowly on. Over the wan, yet lovely face of the sleeper had come a gradual change—agonizing, yet indescribable. It ever appears when Death approaches to claim his victim, and it seems as though the shadow cast by his black pinions. Mary opened her eyes and looked silently on the sad group which clustered around her couch. Mr. Stewart, alone able to command his voice, asked if she was not better, as she had slept so gently.

"All is well, Mr. Stewart—I have no pain;" and her eye again rested on Florence. Long was the look, and full of deep, unutterable tenderness. Feebly she extended her hand.

"Florry!"

Her cousin knelt beside her, and buried her face in her hands. Mary laid hers on the bowed head.

"Dear Florry, I have little time to stay. Do not sadden this last hour with vain regrets. Ah! my cousin, I thank God that you will be so happy. When you miss me from your side you will feel lonely enough, and your heart will ache for me again. Yet, though bodily absent, I shall not be far away, Florry. My spirit will hover round the loved ones I leave on earth. Your dead, forming an angel-guard, will ever linger about your earthly path, and in the hour like this will bear up your spirit to God. Think not of me as resting in the silent grave. I shall not be there, but ever near you. I do not say, try to forget me and fix your thoughts on other things. Oh! I beg you to think of me often, and of our glorious reunion in heaven! Florry, there is one thing which will stand between you and me. **My dear cousin,** conquer your pride, cast away your haughtiness, and learn to lean on God, and walk in accordance with his law. Oh! who would exchange the hope of a Christian for all that worlds could offer? One may pass through life, and do without it; but in the hour of death its claim is imperatively urged, and none can go down to the tomb in peace without it. Florry, you said last night it was hard that I should die. I am not merely reconciled, but I am happy! Earth looks very bright and joyous, and if I might stay, my future is attractive indeed. Yet I know that for some good end I am taken, and what seems to you so hard, is but a blessing in disguise. Oh! then, when you are summoned away, may you feel, as I now do, that the arms of your God are outstretched to receive you." She held out her hand to Mr. Stewart, who stood beside her: he clasped it in his.

"Cherish Florry, and let no shadow come between you. It gives me inexpressible joy to know that when I am gone you will be near to love and to guide her."

"We will comfort and guide each other, dear Mary, and oh! I pray God that we may be enabled to join you in that land of rest to which you are hastening." He fervently kissed the thin white hand he held, and then gently raised Florence. Mary lifted her arms feebly, and they clasped each other in a long, last embrace.

"Mary, my angel cousin, I can not give you up. Oh! I have never prized you as I ought. Who will love me as you have done?"

"Hush, Florry!" whispered the sinking voice of the sufferer. "I am very, very happy—kiss me, and say good-by."

Gently Dr. Bryant took Florence from her cousin, and then each in turn, Mrs. Carlton and Aunt Lizzy, bent over her; as the latter turned away, Mary took her hand, and drawing her down, murmured:

"My dear aunt, forgive what may have pained you in my past life. We have differed on many points, but we both know there is one God. Oh! aunt, in his kingdom may we soon meet again: think of me often, dear aunt. When I am gone you will be very lonely, but only for a short period are we separated."

Dr. Bryant elevated her pillow that she might rest more easily. She lifted her eyes to his pale face. "Frank, will you turn the sofa that I may see the sun set once once more?"

He moved it to the west window, and drew aside the curtain that the golden beams might enter: she could not look out, for the sofa was low, and sitting down beside her, he passed his arm around her, and lifted her head to his bosom. For a time she looked out on the brilliant hues of the setting sun, now just visible above the tree tops. Slowly it sank, then disappeared forever to her vision. Once Dr. Bryant had seen her lips move, as in prayer; now the deep blue eyes were again raised to the loved face bending over her.

"Long ago, I prayed to God that I might fade away gently, and die a painless death. He has granted my petition. All things seem very calm and beautiful—earth ne'er looked so like heaven before; yet how insignificant in comparison with the glories which await me. Frank, if aught could draw me back, and make me loth to leave this world, it would be my love for you. Life would be so bright passed by your side. You know the depth of my love, yet I may not remain. Frank, tell me that you can give me up for a little while. Oh! can you not say, 'God's will be done?'"

"Mary, it is a terrible trial to yield you up, when I looked forward so joyously to the future. It is hard to think of the long, long dreary years that are to come, and know that you will not be near me; that I can not see your face, or hear your loved tones. Oh, Mary, you know not the bitterness of this hour; yet I can say God's will be done, for I have conquered my own heart, but every earthly joy and hope has passed away. To our reunion I must ever look as my only comfort, and I pray God that it may be speedy."

He bent his head till his lips rested on the white brow, now damp in death. Wearily she turned her face toward his; he clasped the wasted form tightly to his heart, and kissed the pale lips; her fingers clasped his hand gently and she whispered, " Good-by?"

"Good-by, my darling Mary!—my own angel one, good-by!"

Again he pressed his lips to hers, and then rested her head more easily upon his arm. The eyes closed, and those who stood watching her low, irregular breathing, fancied she slept again.

One arm was around her, while the other supported the drooping head. Her beautiful brown hair fell over his arm, and left exposed the colorless face. She was wasted, yet beautiful in its perfect peace and joy was the expression which rested on her features. Dr. Bryant, leaning his noble brow on hers, felt her spirit pass away in the last sigh which escaped her lips. Yet he did not lift his head. Cold as marble grew the white fingers which lingered in his, still he clasped her tightly. He sat with closed eyes, communing with his own saddened heart; he was stilling the agony which welled up, and casting forth the bitterness which mingled darkly with his grief, and he said unto his tortured soul: "Be still! my treasure is laid up in heaven."

He lifted the hair from his arm, and gently drew his hand from hers; yet, save for the icy coldness of her brow, none would have known that the soul which lent such gentle loveliness to the countenance had flown home to God.

Dr. Bryant pressed a last kiss on the closed eyes and marble brow, softly laid her on her pillow, and left the room.

CHAPTER XXX.

"ALL things are dark to sorrow," and the very repose of beauty of nature seems to the aching heart a mockery. No violent bursts of grief had followed Mary's death, for so peaceful and painless was her end, it was scarce allowable. Yet now that she had been consigned to the quiet grave, a dreary sense of loneliness and desolation crept to the hearts of the saddened group. They stood assembled at the door of their new home, to bid adieu to Dr. Bryant. In vain had been his sister's tears and entreaties, and Mr. Carlton's expostulations. Florence had clasped his hand, and asked in trembling accents, why he left them in their sorrow, and Mr. Stewart implored him not to seek death on the battle-field.

Firm in his purpose, naught availed. He stood upon the step ready to depart; his noble face was very pale, and grief had touched with saddening finger every lineament. Yet his tone and mien were calm as usual.

"My dear sister," said he, "in times like these a man should first regard duty—the laws and precepts of his God! then the claims of his suffering country; and lastly, the ties of nature and the tenderer feelings of his heart. Ellen, think how many have torn themselves from weeping wives and clinging children, and cast their warm love far from them. The call to patriots is imperative. I have now nothing to detain me here: it is my duty to lend my arm toward supporting our common liberty. Do not fear for me, Ellen, my dear sister; remember that the strong arm of all-seeing God is ever around us, to guard in time of danger!" He clasped her tenderly to his heart, then placed her in her husband's arms.

"Florence, if not again in Texas, I hope we shall soon meet, in more peaceful hours, in Louisiana; if not, I pray God that you and Stewart may be as happy as I once hoped to be." He pressed her hand warmly, and returning the long, tight clasp of Mr. Stewart, mounted his horse and rode slowly away.

"Mother," said Elliot, "Uncle Frank has not taken the right road toward home."

"Hush, Elliot!" she sadly answered, while her tears gushed anew; "he has gone by his Mary's grave."

On that hour, spent at the early tomb of the "loved and lost" Mary, we will not intrude: it is rendered sacred by its deep, unutterable anguish.

Nearly a week passed, and Dr. Bryant had hurried on, riding through the long, long nights, and only pausing at times to recruit his jaded steed. He had arrived at within two days' ride of San Antonio, and too wearied to proceed, stopped as night closed in, and picketing his horse wrapped his cloak about him, and threw himself under a large spreading oak to rest, and, if possible, to sleep. An hour passed on: still he lay looking up to the brilliant sky above. Perfect quiet reigned around, and he felt soothed inexpressibly. Overcome with fatigue, sleep stole on, and momentary oblivion of the past was granted.

He was startled from his slumber by the neighing of his horse; and rising lightly drew forth his pistols, cocked one, and turned in the direction whence came the sound of approaching hoofs. The neighing was answered by the advancing steed, and soon the figure of both rider and horse was dimly seen; for the moon was not yet risen, and the pale light of the stars but faintly assisted the vision.

"Who comes there?" asked Dr. Bryant, throwing off his cloak, and stepping up to the stranger.

"A peaceful Mexican, in search of cows, and some twenty sheep which strayed away. I think, from your voice, you are an Americano. I am friendly to your people—you will not molest me, and I will not harm you."

"My friend, I rather doubt your word. These are stormy times for a man to venture out in search of cattle, so far from San Antonio."

"I could tell you a piece of news that would satisfy you that I run less risk than yourself. But, stranger, it's not civil to doubt a man's word, and make him an enemy whether he will or not."

"I am willing to receive your proffered proof of sincerity, and hope to find you unlike your fickle nation. Come, tell the news which sanctions this long ramble of yours. These are dark days, and it becomes every man to look well to his own safety, and likewise watch his neighbor's movements."

"I will do you a kindness, stranger; turn your horse's head, and let moon-rise find you where you drank water at noon. San Antonio is no place for

Americans now. Santa Anna has taken the Alamo; and all of your people lie low. Not one was spared to carry the tale to Austin—no, not one!"

Dr. Bryant groaned in spirit, and his extended arm sunk to his side.

"O God! hast thou forsaken us? Surely thou wilt yet listen to the voice of justice and liberty," he murmured to himself, and there was a pause.

"How long since the ill-fated Alamo fell?" he inquired.

"Five days ago. Hintzilopotchli came down and held his bloody feast and cut off many brave men."

"By what force was the fortress assaulted?"

"Seven thousand men, led by the great and victorious Santa Anna. Not long lasted the strife: we were too many for your people, and the fight was short."

"And was our noble Travis slaughtered with his brave band?"

"He was too brave to live. Think you he would survive his comrades? No! he fell first, and then all followed."

"Will Santa Anna march to Austin think you; or, content with victory, remain in your town?"

"Truly, you give me credit for few brains and a woman's tongue. I have told you one true tale, can you expect another from a fickle Mexican? I tell you now, stranger, push me not too closely, if you would hear what is good for you."

"Your voice sounds strangely familiar; yet I cannot recognize it sufficiently to know with whom I am speaking. If, as you declare, friendly to our people, you will not object to giving your name. Perhaps I have known you in San Antonio."

"We Mexicans can tell a friend across the prairie —but no matter. I am thinking we be strangers, yet I am not ashamed of my name. They call me Antoine Amedo—did you ever hear of such an 'hombre?' My ranch is just below the mission San Jose, and I have large flocks of sheep and cattle."

"Antoine Amedo," repeated Dr. Bryant, musingly. and striving, through the gloom, to scan his features. "You are right; I do not know you, though your voice is familiar."

"If you have no objection, Señor Americano, I will let my horse picket awhile, and rest myself; for I have ridden many miles since sunrise, and not a 'barego' have I smelled."

"You are at liberty to rest as long as you please: consult your own inclinations." And he turned away to his own horse, yet marked that the new comer dismounted with some difficulty.

He changed his own picket, that fresh grass might not be wanting; and returning to the tree, leaned against its huge body, and watched the movements of the intruder. They were very slow, as if he were well-nigh spent with over-exertion. He took off his broad hat, smoothed his hair, then replaced it; adjusted his heavy blanket more comfortably, and drawing forth a sort of wallet, proceeded to satisfy the cravings of hunger. He ate but little, and returning the bag or sack to its hiding-place in the broad girdle which was passed about his waist beneath the blanket, stretched himself on the ground, with not even a straggling bough between him and the deep blue vault of heaven.

No sound broke the silence, save the cropping of the horses as they grazed near; and, seeking again his grassy couch, Dr. Bryant closed his eyes, and communed with his own heart. Sleep was now impossible, and he lay so rapt in thought, that time flew on unheeded. The moon was shining brightly now, and every object was distinctly seen. He heard the rustling of leaves and the crush of grass. A moment he opened his eyes, then closed them, and feigned sleep.

The Mexican had risen, and softly approaching the motionless form, knelt on the ground beside him, and listened to his breathing. It was low and regular, as one in quiet slumber. He bent and gazed into the up-turned face—not a muscle quivered or a feature moved. Stealthily a hand crept round the collar of the cloak, and lifted a heavy lock of the raven hair. Smoothing it out on the grass, he drew forth a crooked blade, which, in accordance with the custom of his countrymen, ever hung in the girdle passed about the waist. It glittered in the moonlight; and with dexterous hand he cut the lock of hair: then, returning the knife to its resting-place, rose, and noiselessly retreating to his former position, some yards distant, threw himself down to sleep.

Dr. Bryant, fully conscious of every movement,

determined, if possible, to solve this mystery. His pistols were in readiness, and, had violence been attempted, he would have sprung to his feet and defended himself. He waited awhile, then turned, stretched, yawned, and finally rose up. He drew out his watch, the hand pointed to two. He wound it up, and drawing his cap closer about his ears, for the night was cold, approached his companion and stirred him with his foot. No sound or movement indicated consciousness; he stooped and shook him.

"Antoine, Antoine, get up my friend: you don't intend to spend the night here, do you?"

Amedo sat upright, and rubbed his eyes with well-feigned sleepiness: "Well, Señor Americano, what is it—Indians smelling about?"

Dr. Bryant could not repress a smile at the drowsy tone of the ranchero, who scarce five minutes before had crept from his side.

"Upon my word, you seem a match for the seven sleepers of old. Why, man, if Indians had stumbled on you by chance, they had slung your scalp on yonder bough. In times like these men should slumber lightly."

"Very true, Señor; yet mine eyes are heavy, for two moons have seen me riding on. But you are up! wherefore?"

"I proceed on my journey, and wakened you to ask advice and direction, and request your company if it be that we take the same route."

"Jesu Maria! One might think the man had

choice! Why, turn your horse's head, and rest for naught but grass and water."

The Mexican had risen, and in adjusting his blanket, a sudden gust of wind lifted his hat, and it fell to the ground at his feet; he clutched at it convulsively, but it was too late. Dr. Bryant started back in astonishment:

"Inez!"

The head sunk on her bosom, and the hair which had been confined at the back of her head, fell in luxuriant masses to her waist.

"Fearless, yet unfortunate girl! what has led you to this freak?"

A singular group they presented, standing on the broad and seemingly boundless prairie—the March wind moaning through the old oaks, and rustling the brown grass. The moon shone full upon them; Dr. Bryant, with his large cloak wrapt closely about him, and the black cap drawn over his brow—surprise, reproach, pity, and chagrin strangely blended in his gaze. One arm was folded over the broad chest, the other hung by his side. Inez stood just before him, her beautiful head bent so that the black locks well-nigh concealed her features. Her father's large variegated blanket hung loosely about the tall, slender form. At her feet lay the hat, crushed by the extended foot, and quivering in the night wind, her hands tightly clasped.

"Inez, you crouch like a guilty being before me! Surely you have done nothing to blush for. Yet stranger step was never taken by a reasonable being. Inez, raise your head, and tell me what induced you to venture in this desolate region, alone, unprotected and in disguise?"

Inez lifted slowly the once beautiful face, now haggard and pale. Anguish of spirit had left its impress on her dark brow, wrinkled by early care. Mournful was the expression of the large, dark eyes raised to his face:

"Dr. Bryant, I am alone in the wide, wide world —there is none to protect—none to care for me now! My father sleeps by Mañuel's side, in the churchyard, and I am the last of my house. The name of De Garcia, once so proud and honored, will become a by-word for desolation and misery! I have said cursed was the hour of my birth, and I now say blessed is the hour of my last sleep! You see me here from necessity, not choice, for all places would be alike to me now; but I have been driven from my lonely hearth—I dared not stay, I flew to this dreary waste for peace—for protection! There is no rest, no peace for me. Not one is left to whom I can say, guard and keep me from harm! Alone, friendless, in this wide, bitter world!"

"Your language is strangely ambiguous, Inez! Can you not explicitly declare what danger threatens, and believe that all I can do to avert evil will gladly be done?"

"Dr. Bryant, the Padre is my most inveterate enemy! Is not this sufficient to account for my presence here?"

"Unfortunate girl! how have you incurred that man's hatred?"

"It is a long tale and needless to repeat: enough, that he plotted my ruin—that the strong, silent walls of a far-off convent was my destination. And why? That my flocks and lands might enrich his precious church! You look wonderingly upon me; strange language, this, I think you say, for a lamb of his flock. How dare you speak so irreverently of the holy man, consecrated priest of Rome as he is? Dr. Bryant, I am no Catholic, nor have I been since you have known me. It was my policy to appear passive. I attended mass, and sought the confessional, and all the while cursed him in my heart. I watched him, and saved your people from destruction. Would you know how? I heard whispered promises to meet at dead of night. I followed: I saw the meeting between an emmissary of Santa Anna and my godly Padre. At imminent risk I listened to their plot. You were to be kept in ignorance of the powerful force hurrying on to destroy you. Santa Anna was to burst suddenly upon the town, and, ere you could receive reinforcements, capture the Alamo at a blow. Once in his possession, more than one of your people were to be handed over to the tender mercies of my holy confessor. I warned you of your danger, and happily you heeded the signs of the time; else you, too, would now moulder beneath the walls of the Alamo. His prey escaped him, and with redoubled eagerness he sought to consummate my destruction. I was made a prisoner in my own home ere the sod settled on my father's grave! I fled in the midnight hour, and you see me here! Dr. Bryant, I well-nigh cut short the knotted thread of my life; but one thing saved me, else my body would even now whirl along the channel of the river. When I parted from the blue-eyed, sainted Mary, she gave me this book and asked me not only to read but follow its teachings. She clasped my hand, and told me to remember God and the eternity which awaited me, and the judgment of that other, final world. Oh! if there be a heaven and a purgatory! a God and a judge! if I sink to perdition, one alone is to blame. He told me he had power to forgive my sins; that the more completely I obeyed him on earth the more blessed I should be in heaven. Yet I have heard him lie, and seen him set aside the rules of humanity and the laws of God! Mary's Bible tells me 'to keep holy the Sabbath day.' Yet from my childhood, I have seen our Priests at mass on Sabbath morning, and at monte and cock-fights on the evening of the same day! And I have seen them take from the widow, as the burial-fee of her husband, the last cow she possessed. I saw these things and I said there is no God, or he would not suffer such as these to minister as his chosen servants upon the earth. I said in my heart, purgatory is but a lie made to keep pace with their marvellous legends and frequent miracles! There is not a purgatory, or they would fear the retribution in store for them. I had none to teach me aright. I mocked at the thought of religion. I said there is none on the earth—it is merely a system of gain, and all that constitutes the difference is, that some are by nature more of devils, and others gifted with milder hearts. But I saw Mary—pure angel that she is—I saw her with the sick and the dying; she railed not at our priest, as he at her. She carried her Bible to the bed of death, and told them to look to God for themselves. She bade them leave off saint-worship and cling to Jesus as their only Mediator. Peace followed her steps, and much good she would have done, but my Padre interfered, peremptorily ordered all good Papists to shun her as they would an incarnate demon, and frightened many into submission with his marvellous tales and threats of purgatory. I said to myself, if there be truth in God and religion, this Mary walketh in the right path, for like an angel of mercy and light she ever seems. She was the hope, the joy, the blessing of all who knew her. Oh! I will come to you, Mary, and learn of you, and die near, that you may be with me in the hour of rest."

Inez sank on the ground, and burying her face in her arms, rocked herself to and fro. Dr. Bryant had listened to her rambling, incoherent language, like one in a dream, till the name of Mary passed her lips, and then his head sank upon his chest, and he groaned in the anguish of his tortured spirit.

Inez held in one hand the small Bible given at parting; his eye fell upon it, and he stepped nearer to her:

"Inez, the Mary you have loved rests no longer

on earth. She has passed away, and dwells in heaven. She was true to God, and his holy law, and great is her reward. Scarce a week since I laid her in her quiet grave, yet not there either, but yielded her up the arms of God!"

He paused, for his deep tone faltered. Inez rose quickly to her feet as he spoke, and gazed vacantly on his face.

"Mary gone forever! Mary in heaven! Shall I never again see her, sweet angel of truth and purity, with her soft blue eyes, so full of holy love and gentleness? Oh, Mary, thou art blessed! thou art at rest! When shall I, too, find eternal rest? Ere long, Mary, I, too, will sleep the last, unbroken, dreamless sleep!"

Dr. Bryant laid his hand on the sacred volume, and would have drawn it from her clasp; but tightening her hold, she shook her head, and mournfully exclaimed:

"No, no; it is mine! When I die, it shall be my pillow; while I live, it rests near my heart, and in the church-yard I will not let it go. You have no right to claim it: you have not loved her as I have done. She loved you, yet you needed not the jewel that might have, even now, been your own!"

"Inez, I have loved—I do love her, as none other can! Too late I found my love returned. Had God spared her to me, she would have been my wife. Oh, Mary, Mary! my own cherished one? May thy spirit hover round me now, as in life thou wert my guardian angel! Inez, I, too, have suffered, and severely. I have little to anticipate in life, yet I am not desponding as you, my faith in God and his unchanging goodness is unshaken. Let us both so live that we may join my Mary in glory."

Inez answered not, but passed her hand wearily across her brow.

"Inez, which will you do? retain your disguise, and go with me, or return to your old home? I am not going to Austin, but to Goliad, to join the Texans there; will you accompany me, and claim the protection of our banner? All that a brother could, I will gladly do; with me you are safe, at least for a time; and when the storm of war has passed, I doubt not your home will again be happy."

"I know you, Dr. Bryant, and I know that you are true to God, and keep his law. I will go with you to Goliad, and there we will decide what I must do. Oh! I am weary and sick at heart, and not long will I burden you."

She stooped, and picking up the hat, replaced it on her head, and turned toward her horse.

Frank kindly took her hand.

"Inez, do not despond. I trust all may yet be well with you, and rest assured it gives me heartfelt pleasure to be enabled to render you a service, and take you to a place of safety. But your hand is hot —burning: it is feverish excitement from which you suffer. When we have reached Goliad, and you can rest, I doubt not your strength and spirits will return; meantime take one of my pistols, it is loaded, and, in case of danger, will render good service."

She took the proffered weapon, and having secured it in the girdle turned to mount her horse. Frank assisted in arranging the accoutrements, and, springing upon his own spirited steed, they turned their faces southward.

CHAPTER XXXI.

> "Our bosoms we'll bare to the glorious strife,
>   And our oath is recorded on high,
> To prevail in the cause that is dearer than life,
>   Or crushed in its ruins to die.
>   *   *   *   *   *
> And leaving in battle no blot on his name,
> Look proudly to heaven, from the death-bed of fame."
>   *Campbell.*

A BLOODY seal was set upon thee, oh! Goliad. A gory banner bound around thy name; and centuries shall slowly roll ere thou art blotted from the memory of man. The annals of the dim and darkened past afford no parallel for the inhuman deed, so calmly, so deliberately committed within thy precincts; and the demon perpetrator escaped unpunished! A perfect appreciation of the spirit of the text, "Vengeance is mine, saith the Lord; I will repay," alone can sanction the apathy manifested by one to whom the world looked as the avenger of his murdered countrymen.

Rumors of the fall of the Alamo, the overwhelming force of Santa Anna, and his own imminent danger, had reached Colonel Fanning. In vain he entreated reinforcements, in vain urged the risk hourly incurred. The Texan councils bade him save himself by flight. "Retreat, fly from the post committed to my keeping!" The words sounded like a knell on the ear of the noble man to whom they were addressed. He groaned in the anguish of his spirit, "I will not leave this fortress—Travis fell defending with his latest breath the Alamo! Oh, Crocket! Bowie! can I do better than follow your example, and give my life in this true cause?"

An untimely death—the separation and misery of his darling family, weighed not an atom! "Patria infelici fidelis!" was ever his motto, and unfaltering was his own step. There came a messenger from headquarters—"Abandon Goliad, and retreat!"

"Colonel, you will not sound a retreat?" and Dr. Bryant laid his hand upon his commander's arm.

"My God! it is a fearful thing to decide the destinies of four hundred brave men! Bryant, if we remain it is certain death—the tragedy of San Antonio will be re-acted in our case!"

"Colonel, you must remember the old saw—'He that fights and runs away, lives to fight another day,'" said a time-worn ranger, settling his collar with perfect nonchalance.

"Why, Furgeson, do you counsel flight? My brave comrade, bethink yourself!"

"Well, Colonel, it is something strange for me to

say run; but when I do say it, I am in earnest. The most hot-headed fellow in our company dare not say I lack courage: you know as well as I do what they call me—'Bull-dog Furgeson;' but who feels like fighting the grand devil himself, and his legion of imps to boot? I am a lone man, and have nothing in particular to live for, it's true; but it is some object with me to do the most service I can for our Lone blessed Star! I should like a game with old "Santy in a clear ring, and fair play; but I am thinking we had best take French leave of this place, and join the main body, where we can fight with some chance ahead. Now that's my opinion, but if you don't believe that doctrine, and want to take the 'old bull right by the horns,' I say lets at him."

A smile passed over the face of his commander.

"Thank you, Furgeson, and rest assured I shall not doubt your stanch support in time of need."

Again the broad brow contracted, and, linking his arm in that of Dr. Bryant, he paced to and fro, engrossed in earnest, anxious thought. Pausing at length, he pointed to his troops, awaiting in silence his commands.

Bryant, at least half those brave fellows have wives and children, and bright homes, beckoning them away, yet see them calmly trust to me in this trying hour. Should my order go forth to man the fort, and meet the worst, I know full well not a murmur would be heard. Still it is equally certain that, if we brave the conflict, not one of us shall survive to tell the tale. What am I to do? Make this a second Thermopylæ?"

" Peculiarly painful, I know full well is the situation in which you are placed. Yet one strong argument remains to be urged. Colonel, if we desert Goliad, and sound a retreat, we can not escape. The force of the enemy is too powerful, their movements too rapid, to allow us to retire to a place of safety without a desperate encounter. Is it not better policy to remain here, and meet the shock?"

" If we fight at all it must be at fearful odds; four hundred to six thousand! Yet, should I follow the dictates of my own heart, I would not give one inch! —no, not one! Dearly they should buy the ground on which I stand!"

" Colonel, shall we not meet them on this spot, and lay down our lives, as did our brethren of the Alamo?"

" No, by Jove! I shall have to leave, whether I will or not!" And crumpling the note of orders, he tossed it to the ground, and pressed it with his heel.

He stepped forth, and drawing his military cap about his eyes, folded his arms upon his broad chest, and addressed his troops:

" Comrades! Retreat is no test of an army's bravery, neither the courage of its commander. In every age and nation, circumstances have occurred in which the cause of liberty, or the general welfare of the state, has been promoted by timely flight rather than desperate engagements. ' The Swamp Fox ' often retired to his island of refuge, safe from invading bands—the daring Sumter was forced at times to retreat; and even our great Washington fled from superior forces, and waited till a more convenient season. Fellow-soldiers: there is one of two steps to be immediately taken. We will stand to our post, and fall to a man, like Travis and his noble band, and our names will go down to posterity as did the Spartans of old,

'Wreathed with honor, and immortal fame ;'

or else we set out at once for head-quarters, consolidate our forces, and march united to oppose Santa Anna.

"Comrades, what shall we do?"

No sound was heard along the ranks, each bent his head and communed with his own spirit; and the image of their distant, yet cherished homes, rose up and murmured—" Remember thy weeping wife and thy fair-browed boy; who will guard them when thou art gone ?"

The eagle eye of their brave leader was piercingly bent on the mute assemblage; the momentary gleam of hope that lighted his noble countenance faded away. There came a faint sound of rising voices— it swelled louder, and louder still:

"God bless our noble Colonel! our brave Fanning! With him is the issue. Say but the word, and we will follow!"

"Bryant, I can not sign their death-warrant!" he said, in a low, subdued tone, sinking his head upon his breast. He lifted himself up, and raising his voice, calmly replied:

"Had I not received orders to retreat, and if I were not fully aware that lingering here insured our total destruction, I should scorn to turn my back upon Goliad! Oh! gladly I would die in its defense; but your fate is too entirely in my hands to admit of following my individual wishes! None know the pang it causes me to sound a 'Retreat,' yet it may be, that the success of our cause demands it at my hands, and therefore I say, ' Retreat, comrades !"—at dawn to-morrow, we move from Goliad."

The decree went forth, and the ensuing day saw the doomed band moving eastward toward headquarters they were destined never to reach.

On arriving at Goliad, Dr. Bryant had immediately enlisted, after placing Inez in safety at the house of an aged Señora of her nation; and no sooner was it decided to leave the town the following day than he sought his Spanish friend.

She was sitting alone when he entered, and quickly rising, placed a seat for him.

" Thank you, Inez, I have only a moment to remain—I come to say good-by."

" Which way do your people go now ?" she hoarsely asked.

"Santa Anna is marching with overwhelming forces toward us, and Colonel Fanning thinks it advisable to retire to headquarters. We set out at dawn to-morrow."

" You cannot escape by flight; it were better to

remain here. I tell you now, if you leave Goliad you will be cut off to a man."

"Inez, my own feelings would strongly incline me to follow your advice, but it has been decided otherwise!"

"Then, if you must go, I go with you!"

"Impossible, Inez, impossible! you know not what you say! For you to venture from this place under existing circumstances, beset as we are on every hand with dangers seen and unseen, would be the height of madness."

"I know not fear! of that you must have been convinced long ere this. Danger cannot intimidate me; what you meet and suffer, that will I encounter."

"Bethink yourself, Inez! What can you hope to accomplish by this strange step? You have nothing to fear here from your own nation: what can you gain by seeking a home among my people? Strange, mysterious being, I wish for your own sake you were timid—that fear might strengthen your sense of prudence!"

Inez had bent her head while he spoke, as in humiliation, now she lifted herself and said, in a low, determined tone:

"I am alone in the wide world, and I have but one hope, but one pleasure; to be with you while life remains, and to die near, that you may close my eyes and lay me down to rest." She paused a moment, and then clasping her hands, approached him, and continued in a more passionate tone:

"Oh, if you knew how I have loved you, you could not look down so coldly, so calmly upon me! you could not refuse the favor I ask! Oh, Dr. Bryant, do not scorn me for my love!—'tis not a common love; for it I have lost every earthly comfort and blessing; for this struggled and toiled, and braved numberless dangers. I have loved you better than every thing beside! Turn not from me, nor think contemptuously of the worship given unsought! If you cannot love me, do not, oh, do not despise me! Let me a little while longer be with you, and see you; I will not trouble or incommode any one—do not leave me. Oh, Dr. Bryant, do not leave me!"

The large black eyes were raised entreatingly to his, and an expression of the keenest anguish rested on her colorless, yet beautiful face.

Sadly he regarded her as she hurried on: no glance of scorn rested even for a moment upon her. Yet a stern sorrow settled on his broad brow, and around the firmly-compressed lips.

"Inez, I do not, cannot love you, other than as the kind friend of other days. I have never loved but one—I never shall. Mary, my own angel Mary, ever rests in my heart. I cannot forget her—I can never love another. I do not even thank you for your love, for your avowal gives me inexpressible pain! I have suspected this, Inez, for long, and your own heart will tell you I gave no ground to hope that I could return your affection. I have striven to treat you like a sister of late, yet this painful hour has not been averted. Equally painful to both. Inez, your own words make it more than ever necessary that we should part forever. I cannot return your love—I will not encourage it. You must, as soon as safety allows, return to your old home. Inez, do not cherish your affection for me, it can only bring pain and remorse; forget me, and remember that you have imperative duties of your own to perform. This is your darkest hour, and believe me, in time you will be happy, and a blessing to your people. Remember Mary's words, and her parting gift, and I pray God that we may so live that we shall all meet in a happier home."

"Then I shall never see you again?" she said, in a calm and unfaltering voice.

"For your sake, Inez, it is best that we should not meet again. If I survive this war I go to Europe, and you will probably never see me more. Inez, I pain you—forgive me. Your own good requires this candor on my part."

An ashy paleness overspread the cheek and brow of his companion as he spoke, and the small hands clutched each other tightly, yet no words passed the quivering lips.

"Good-by, Inez! my kind and valued friend, good-by!" He held out his hand. She raised her head, and gazed into the sad yet noble face of the man she had loved so long. She clasped his hand between both hers, and a moan of bitter anguish escaped the lips.

"My love will follow you forever! A woman of my nature cannot forget. I shall sink to eternal rest with your name on my lips—your image in my heart. Yet I would not keep you here—go, and may your God ever bless you, and—and—may you at last meet your Mary, if there be a heaven! We part now, for you have said it; good-by, and sometimes, when all is joy and gladness to you, think a moment on Inez! the cursed, the miserable Inez! sitting in bitter darkness by her lonely hearth! Good-by!" She pressed her lips to his hand, and without a tear, shrouded her face in her mantilla and turned away.

"God bless you, Inez, and keep you from all harm!" and Dr. Bryant left the house, and returned to his commander.

Colonel Fanning had led his troops but a few miles when the vanguard halted, and some excitement was manifested. Spurring forward, he inquired the cause of delay.

"Why, Colonel, if we ain't 'out of the frying-pan into the fire,' my name is not Will Furgeson. Look yonder, Colonel, it takes older and weaker eyes than mine to say them ain't Santy Anna's imps marching down upon us, thick as bees just swarmed too!"

"You are right, Furgeson; it is the entire Mexican force! let us form at once and meet them!"

Quickly and clearly his orders rang out, and his little band, compact and firm, waited in silence the result. With an exulting shout the Mexicans charged. Desperately the doomed Texans fought, heaping up the slain at every step. The wily Santa Anna changed his tactics. There came a momentary cessation as the crowding thousands were furiously driven back. And, seizing the opportunity, he spurred forward, offered honorable terms, and besought Fanning to surrender and save the lives of his brave followers.

"We will only surrender on condition that every privilege of prisoners of war be guaranteed to us," replied Colonel Fanning.

"I, Santa Anna, commander-in-chief of the Mexican force, do most solemnly pledge my word, that all the privileges consistent with your situation as prisoners of war, shall be extended to yourself and men. And hereby swear, that on these conditions you may lay down your arms in safety, without further molestation on our part."

Is there one of my readers, who, for a moment, would attach blame to the noble Fanning? The lives of his men were of far more importance to him than the renown of perishing, like Travis, in a desperate struggle. With the latter there was no alternative, for the cry of even seven exhausted men for " quarter " was disregarded, and the garrison fell to a man. But honorable terms were offered Fanning; he remembered his men, and surrendered. Santa Anna! can there be pardon for such a hardened wretch as you? Does not sleep fly your pillow? In the silent watches of the night, do not the spectre forms of your victims cluster about your couch, and the shambles of Goliad rise before you? Can you find rest from the echoing shrieks of murdered thousands, or shut your eyes and fail to perceive the mangled forms stiffening in death and weltering in gore ? If you are human, which I much doubt, your blackened soul will be tortured with unavailing remorse, till Death closes your career on earth, and you are borne to the tribunal of Almighty God, there to receive your reward. . . .

Night found the Texans again in Goliad, and they sought sleep secure from evil; for had not Santa Anna's word been given that further molestation would not be allowed? and they believed! Soundly they slept, and dreamed of far-off homes and fireside joys.

" That bright dream was their last !"

Sunrise came, and they were drawn out upon the Plaza. Their leader was retained in custody, and, unsuspicious of harm, they each maintained their position. Dr. Bryant raised his eyes—they rested for a moment on Santa Anna's face. Turning quickly, he shouted aloud,

" Turn, comrades, let us not be shot in the back!"

Another moment the signal was given, and a deadly fire poured upon four hundred unresisting prisoners of war, to whom honorable conditions had been granted by the brave and noble generalissimo of the Mexican forces.

Not one of many noble forms was spared. Dr. Bryant sank without a struggle to the earth; and his spirit, released from sorrowing mortality, sprang up to meet his Mary and his God!

The deed was done; and Santa Anna, the mighty

chief who mowed down four hundred unarmed men was immortalized! Fear not, brave hearts, that posterity will forget you! Rest assured that the lapse of time can not obliterate the memory of your mighty deeds!

Fanning survived but a few hours, and then a well-aimed ball laid low forever his noble head. Who among us can calmly remember that his body was denied a burial? Oh, thou martyr leader of a martyr band, we cherish thy memory! dear to the heart of every Texan, every American, every soldier and every patriot. Peace to thee, noble Fanning!

It was noon! Still and cold lay the four hundred forms upon the Plaza. Even as they sank, so they slept. No disturbing hand had misplaced one stiffened member. The silence of death reigned around the murdered band. A muffled figure swiftly stole down the now deserted streets, and hurrying to the Plaza, paused and gazed on the ruin and wreck that surrounded her. Pools of blood were yet standing, and the earth was damp with gore. One by one Inez turned the motionless forms, still the face she sought was not to be found. She had almost concluded her search when her eyes fell on a prostrate form, closely wrapt in a long black cloak; she knelt and gazed into the upturned face, and a low cry of bitter anguish welled up and passed her colorless lips. Gently she lifted the cloak, clasped by one icy hand; the ball had pierced his side and entered the heart. So instantaneous had been his death that not a feature was convulsed. The dark clustering hair was borne back from the broad white brow, the eyes closed as in deep sleep, the finely-cut lips just parted. Pallid was the cheek, yet calm and noble beyond degree was the marble face on which Inez gazed. She caught the cold hand to her lips, and laid her cheek near his mouth, that she might know and realize that his spirit had indeed joined Mary's in the "land of rest." The icy touch extinguished every gleam of hope, and calmly she drew the cloak over the loved face, concealing every feature, then dropped her handkerchief upon the covered head, and drawing her mantilla like a shroud about her, went her way to wait for night and darkness.

Stretched on a couch in the home of the kind-hearted Señora who had received her, Inez noted the moments and hours as they passed. An eternity seemed comprised in the time which elapsed from noon till dusk. Again and again she raised her bowed head and looked out on the slowly sinking sun. It passed at length beyond her vision. She rose and sought her friend, an aged dame, whom God had gifted with a gentle heart, keenly alive to the grief and sufferings of another.

"Well, Señora Inez, what will you have?"

"I have a great favor to ask, yet it is one I doubt not will be granted. Señora, among yonder slain is one who in life was ever kind to me and to our people. Since morning he has lain in his own blood! To-morrow will see them thrown into heaps, and left with scarce sod enough to cover! I cannot, will not see him buried so! I myself will lay him down to rest, if Santa Anna claims my life for it to-morrow! I have caused a grave to be dug in a quiet spot, but I cannot bear him to it unassisted. My strength is gone—I am well-nigh spent: will you help me to-night? They will not miss him to-morrow, and none will know till all is at rest! Señora, will you come with me?"

- "Tell me first, Inez, if it is he who brought you here; who acted so nobly to me, and bade adieu to you but two days since?"

"Yes, the same! will you refuse to assist me now?"

"No, by our blessed Virgin! I will do all an old woman like me can do; yet united, Inez, we shall be strong."

Wrapping their mantillas about them, they noiselessly proceeded to the Plaza. Darkness had closed in, and happily they met not even a straggling soldier, for all, with instinctive dread, shunned the horrid scene. They paused as Señora Berara stumbled over a dead body, and well nigh slipped in blood:

"Jesu Maria! my very bones ache with horror! this is no place for me. Señorita, how will you keep the body? Oh! let us make haste to leave here!"

"Hush! do you see a white spot gleaming yonder? Nay, don't clutch my arm, it is only my handkerchief. I laid it there to mark the place. Come on, step lightly, or you will press the dead."

With some difficulty they made their way along

the damp, slippery ground, now and then catching at each other for support. Inez paused on reaching her mark, and bent down for several moments; then raising herself she whispered:

"Señora, I have wrapped his cloak tightly about him, lift the corners near his feet, while I carry his head. Be careful, lift gently, and do not let the cloak slip."

Slowly they lifted the motionless form, and steadily bore it away: Inez taking the lead, and stepping cautiously. She left the Plaza and principal streets, and turned toward a broad desolate waste, stretching away from the town, and bare, save a few gnarled oaks that moaned in the March wind. The moon rose when they had proceeded some distance beyond the last house, and Inez paused suddenly, and looked anxiously about her.

"Sacra Dio! I trust you have not lost your way! Holy mother, preserve us if we have gone wrong."

"I knew we must be near the place: it is under yonder tree; fear nothing, Señora, come on:" and a few more steps brought them to the designated spot.

A shallow excavation had been made, sufficient to admit with ease the body of a full-grown man; and on its margin they softly laid their burden down. Every object shone in the clear moonlight, and stranger scene never moon shown upon. A dreary waste stretched away in the distance, and sighingly the wind swept over it. Inez knelt beside the grave, her wan yet still beautiful features convulsed with the secret agony of her tortured soul; the long raven hair floating like a black vail around the wasted form. Just before her stood the old woman, wierd-like, her wrinkled, swarthy face exposed to full view, while the silver hair, unbound by her exertion, streamed in the night breeze. Loosely her clothes hung about her, and the thin, bony hands were clasped tightly as she bent forward and gazed on the marble face of the dead. Wonder, awe, fear, pity, all strangely blended in her dark countenance.

Inez groaned, and rocked herself to and fro, as if crushed in body and spirit. She could not lay him to rest forever without the bitterest anguish, for in life she had worshiped him, and in death her heart clung to the loved form. Again and again she kissed the cold hand she held.

"Señorita, we must make haste to lay him in, and cover him closely. Don't waste time weeping now; you can not give him life again. Have done, Señorita Inez, and let us finish our work."

" I am not weeping, Señora! I have not shed a single tear; yet be patient: surely there is yet time."

Inez straightened the cloak in which Frank Bryant was shrouded, placed the hands calmly by his side, and softly smoothed the dark hair on his high and noble brow. She passionately kissed the cold lips once, then covered forever the loved, loved features, and they carefully lowered the still form into its last resting-place.

They stood up, and the old dame pointed to the earth piled on either side. Inez shuddered and closed her eyes a moment, as if unequal to the task.

Her companion stooped, and was in the act of tossing forward a mass of earth; but Inez interposed: "Señora, softly! I will do this: remember there is no coffin."

Fearfully calm was her tone as she slowly pushed in the earth. There was no hollow echo, such as ofttimes rends the heart of the mourner, but a heavy, dull sound of earth crushing earth. Gradually she filled the opening even with the surface, then carefully scattered the remaining sod.

"I will not raise a mound, for they would tear him up should they know where I have lain him." Inez walked away, and gathering a quantity of brown, shriveled leaves, and also as much grass as she could draw from the short bunches, sprinkled them on the grave and along the fresh earth.

"Think you, Señora, they will find him here?"

"No, no, Señorita! none will know that we have buried him. But the night is already far gone, why do you linger?"

For a moment longer Inez gazed down upon the new-made grave: "But a few more hours, and I shall sleep here by your side; farewell till then."

She turned away, and silently they retraced their steps to the town, reaching without inquiry or molestation their own home.

CHAPTER XXXII.

"So live, that when thy summons comes to join
 The innumerable caravan, that moves
 To the pale realms of shade, where each shall take
 His chamber in the silent walls of death,
 Thou go not, like the quarry slave, at night
 Scourged to his dungeon; but sustained and soothed
 By an unfaltering trust, approach thy grave
 Like one who wraps the drapery of his couch
 About him, and lies down to pleasant dreams."
 —*Bryant.*"

A BRIGHT day in April drew near its close, and the golden rays of the spring sun poured joyously through the open casement into the chamber of death. Yes, the " King of Terrors " drew nigh, and the cold damp, which his black pinions swept on, settled upon the brow of Inez. A few days after the massacre at Goliad, a raging fever crimsoned her cheeks, and lent unwonted brilliance to the large black eyes. Delirium ensued, and wildly the unfortunate girl raved of the past—of her former love, her hopelessness, her utter desolation. The dreamless sleep of exhaustion followed this temporary madness; long she lay in the stupor so near akin to death, and now, consciousness restored, she awaited in silence her hour! In vain the kind-hearted Señora entreated her to see a priest—steadfastly she refused. At length Madame Berara assumed the responsibility of calling in her own confessor, and silently quitting the room, went in quest of him. Inez suspected the cause of her unusual absence, and too feeble to concentrate her thoughts, turned her face to the wall, and wearily closed her eyes. Yet one hand felt along the cover and beneath the pillow. For what was she searching on the bed of death? The thin fingers rested on a small and well-worn Bible, and a tiny package, wrapped in paper and carefully tied. The sacred volume was feebly pushed beneath her head, and mechanically she undid the knot, and drew forth a glossy lock of black hair. Wearily she pressed it to her lips several times, and again folding it away, her hands sank powerless upon her bosom.

Señora Berara re-entered the silent chamber, accompanied by a priest, clad in the vestments of his order. They approached the bed, and the aged dame, bending over Inez, whispered audibly:

"I could not find my own Padre, but I bring one who will confess and absolve thee! Make haste to prepare for heaven."

"I want neither confession nor absolution! Begone! and let me die in peace," she answered, without unclosing the lids, which lay so heavily upon the sunken eyes.

"Leave us together! I will call thee when thou art wanted," whispered he of the Order of Jesus. The matron immediately withdrew, repeating an Ave Maria; and they were left alone.

"Inez!"

A shudder crept through the wasted form, and, with a start, she looked upon the face of the intruder. Even in death, hatred was strong; the dim eye flashed, and the cold, damp lips wreathed into a smile of utter scorn:

"Well, Padre, you have tracked me at last! It is a pity, though, you had not set out one day later; you would have altogether missed your prey! But I am content, for I am far beyond your reach!" She gasped for breath, yet ghastly was the mocking smile which lit up her face.

"Not so, Inez! you escaped me once; I have you now! You have defied me in health; but in death I conquer. You cannot die in peace without my blessing. Remember, remember, one sin unconfessed will sink you into everlasting perdition! Think you I will absolve you? Never! never!"

"What brings you here? Think you the approach of death will terrify me?—that I shall claim your intercession and absolution! Have you come hoping to make a bargain, and receive my order for a hundred sheep, or as many cattle, on condition that you pray me out of purgatory? I tell you now, if there be such a place, you will surely follow me ere long. We shall not be separated long, my godly Padre!"

Large drops rolled from her brow, and, gasping, she continued more indistinctly:

"There is one to stand between us now, even black-browed Death! and now, as I speak, I see his shadow flung over me. I am dying, and if I am

lost, you are to blame! you, and you only! You a
man of God! You forgive my sins, and give me a
passport to heaven! Padre, I know you, in all your
hypocrisy, and I know that, if there be a God, you
have outraged his every law! You have led me
astray! You have brought me to this! Padre, I
am sinful, full well I know it; for this is an hour
when the barrier which hides the secret soul is
thrown down, and every deed and thought stands up
boldly for itself. I have not served God! But oh!
I would not change places with you, leader, teacher,
guide, consecrated priest, as you are—for you have
mocked him! Yes, mocked him! set aside his written word, and instead of Bible truths you told me of
Saints, and Relics, and Miracles! You bade me
worship the cross, and never once mentioned Him
who consecrated it with his agony and blood! In
my childhood I believed your legends and miracles,
and trusted such as you to save me. A dreadful
curse will rest upon your head, for you came in
sheep's clothing, and devoured many precious souls,
Padre, I—I—" In vain she strove to articulate, further utterance was denied her. The ghastly hue of
death settled upon her face. She lifted her eyes to
heaven as in prayer; vacantly they wandered to the
face of the Padre, now well-nigh as pale as her own,
then slowly closed forever. A slight quiver passed
over the lips, a faint moan, and Inez was at rest. For
long her wearied spirit had cried "Peace! peace!"
and now she laid herself down and slept the long,
unbroken sleep of death.

> "Oh! you have yearned for rest,
> May you find it in the regions of the blest."

As she had died without the pale of the church, they refused the lifeless form a narrow bed in consecrated ground. Even the ordinary service for the dead was entirely omitted; and, without a prayer, they committed her to the silent tomb. The kind old dame, remembering her grief at the secret burial of her noble friend, obtained permission to lay her by his side, and, with the fierce howlings of the tempest for her funereal dirge, they consigned Inez—the proud, beautiful, gifted, yet unfortunate Inez—to rest. Peace, Inez, to thy memory, and may the sod lie lightly on thy early grave!

CHAPTER XXXIII.

> "There's a bliss beyond all that the minstrel has told,
> When two, that are linked with one heavenly tie,
> With heart never changing, and brow never cold,
> Love on through all ills, and love on till they die!"
> —*Moore.*

"COME, Florence, put on your bonnet; we land in a few moments," said Mr. Stewart, entering the splendidly furnished saloon of a Mississippi steamer, where she sat, book in hand. Quietly the young wife, for such she now was, complied with his request, and taking her husband's arm, they advanced to the bow of the boat. It was a bright, sunny morning in early May, and the balmy breath of the opening summer wafted gladness to many a weary, aching heart. The margin of the river was fringed with willow, poplar, cotton-wood and cypress, the delicate fresh green foliage contrasting beautifully with the deep azure sky, and the dark whirling waters of the turbid stream. It was such a day as all of us may have known, when nature wore the garb of perfect beauty, and the soothing influence is felt and acknowledged by every one accustomed from childhood duly to appreciate, admire, and love the fair and numberless works of God, who,

> ———"Not content
> With every food of life to nourish man,
> Makes all nature beauty to his eye
> And music to his ear."

Florence was gazing intently, as each object receded from her view. They turned an angle in the stream and drew near a landing with only a solitary warehouse visible. She started, and her clasped hands resting on her husband's arm, pressed heavily. He looked down into the flushed face, and said, with a smile:

"Well, Florence, what is it? Why do you tremble so?"

"Mr. Stewart, I can not be mistaken; this is my father's old landing! Why do you look so strangely! Oh! if you knew what painful memories crowd upon my mind you could not smile so calmly!" and her voice faltered.

Laying his hand tenderly on hers, he replied:

"You once asked me whereabouts on the river my plantation was situated. I evaded your question. You are aware that I inherited it from a bachelor uncle. He purchased it from your father, and to your old home, my dear Florence, we have come at last. It is yours again, and I should have told you long ago but feared you might be impatient of the journey: and then it is pleasant to surprise you."

Ere Florence could speak the mingled emotions of her heart, the boat stopped, and the jangling bells warned them to lose no time.

Mr. Stewart placed her on the bank, and beckoning to a coachman mounted on a large heavy carriage, opened the door, assisted her in, and then cordially shaking the outstretched hand of the servant, inquired if all were well at home?"

"Oh yes, sir! all well except your mother. She has had the asthma, but is better. But ain't you going to let me look at your wife? You put her in as if I wan't to see my new mistress."

Mr. Stewart laughed, and opening the door, bade Florence look out; she threw back her long mourning veil, and bent forward; their eyes met, and both started with surprise.

"Isaac!"

"Miss Florry! sure as I am alive!" and he grasped the white hand heartily.

"I cannot understand this at all! Isaac, how came you here?"

"Why, you see, when the plantation was sold, we were sold with it; that's how I came to be here."

"My dear Florence, it is strange, very strange, that I never once thought of your recognizing the servants, though I should have known you could not forget them. In what capacity did Isaac formerly serve?"

"He was always our coachman; and many a ride in childhood I owe to his kindness and wish to make me happy. Isaac, I am very glad to see you again." And her smile confirmed her words.

Mr. Stewart took the seat by her side, and was closing the door, when the old man interfered.

"Miss Florry, I know old master is dead—we heard that some time ago; but where is Miss Mary? that blessed good child, that never gave a cross word to one on the plantation. Why didn't she come home with you?"

Florence could not reply, and the tears rolled silently over her cheeks.

"Isaac," said Mr. Stewart, in a low, saddened tone, "Mary has gone to a brighter home in heaven! She is happier far than she could be even here with us! She died about a month ago."

There was a pause, and then, wiping his rough sleeve across his eyes, Isaac slowly said—"And Miss Mary is dead! Well, she has gone to heaven, if ever any body did! for she was never like common children. Many's the time when my poor little Hannah was burnt, and like to die, that child has come by herself of dark nights to bring her a cake, or something sweet and good! God bless her little soul' she always was an angel!" and again wiping his eyes he mounted the box and drove homeward.

Ah! gentle Mary! no sculptured monument marks thy resting-place! No eulogistic sermon, no high-flown panegyric was ever delivered on thy life and death! Yet that silent tear of old Isaac's outspoke a thousand eulogies! It told of all thy kindness, charity, love, angelic purity of heart, and called thee "Guardian Angel" of the house of Hamilton.

Night found Florence sitting alone in the parlor of her old and dearly loved home. The apartment was much as she had left it five years before, and old familiar articles of furniture greeted her on every side. She sat down to the piano, on which in girlhood she had practiced, and gently touched the keys The soft tones, waking the "slumbering chord of memory," brought most vividly back the scenes of other days. Again she stood there, an only cherished daughter, and her father's image as he used to stand leaning against the mantle-piece, rose with startling distinctness before her. And there, too, stood her cousin, with the soft blue eyes and golden curls of her girlhood; and she fancied she heard, once again, the clear, sweet voice, and felt the fond twining of her arms about her. Long forgotten circumstances in primitive freshness rushed upon her mind, and unable to bear the sad associations which crowded up, Florence turned away from the instrument, and seating herself on the sofa, gave vent to an uncontrollable burst of sorrow——

> "Oh! what a luxury it is to weep,
> And find in tears a sad relief!"

And calmly Florence wept, not bitterly, for she had had much of sorrow to bear, and schooled her heart to meet grief and sadness. Yet it was hard to come back to her cherished home and miss from her side the gentle playmate of her youth, the parent she had almost idolized, and feel that she had left them in far distant resting-places. She heard her husband's step along the hall, and saw him enter—she strove to repress her tears and seem happy, but the quivering lips refused to smile. He sat down, and drawing his arm around her, pressed her face to his bosom, and tenderly said:

"My mother had much to say, after my long absence, and I could not leave her till this moment. My own heart told me that you suffered, and I longed to come to you and sympathize and cheer."

"Do not think me weak, Mr. Stewart, because you find me weeping. It is seldom I give vent to my feelings, but to-night I am overwhelmed with recollections of the past. Oh! now, for the first time, I realize Mary has indeed gone forever. Mary! Mary! my heart aches already for you, and your warm, unchanging love! Oh! how can I look forward to the long coming years, and feel that I shall never see her again?"

"Florence, my own Florence, I would not have you repress a single tear. I know how sadly altered all things are, and what a dreary look your home must bear. All I ask is, that when you feel lonely and unhappy, instead of hiding your grief, come to me, lay your weary head upon my shoulder, and I will strive to cheer you, my precious wife! Let nothing induce you to keep aught from me—let perfect confidence reign between us; and do not, for a moment, doubt that I wish you other than you are. The past is very painful both to you and to me, and the memory of Frank and Mary constantly saddens my spirit. Yet we will look forward to a happier future, and strive to guide and cheer each other." He kissed the broad brow as he spoke, and drew tighter the arm which encircled his wife, as though no danger could assail while he was near.

"Of late, Mr. Stewart, I have wondered much how you ever learned to love me; for I am much changed, and in my girlhood I was cold, proud, and often contemptuous in my manner. Ah, Mary, how different from you! If I have higher aims in life, and purer joys, I owe it all to her, for she led me to love the law of God, and exemplified in her daily life the teachings of Christ! But for her, I shudder to think what I should now have been. O God, I thank thee that I am saved even as a burning brand from the fire! I have hope of happiness on earth, and at last a joyful reunion with the loved ones that have gone on home before me. And you, my husband, help me to conquer myself, to break down my pride, and to be more like Mary. Oh forgive my weakness, and ever love me as you now do!"

He clasped her to his heart, and whispered—" Fear not, Florence, that I will ever love you less! I, too, have faults which you may be called on to excuse, yet all is bright for us, and I trust no common share of happiness will be our portion through life!"

> "Oh, sweet reward of danger past!
> How lovely, through the tears
> That speak her heart's o'erflowing joy,
> The young wife's smile appears.
> The fount of love for her hath gushed,
> Life's shadows all have flown;
> Joy, Florence! thou a heart hast found
> Responding to thine own!"

THE END.

www.ingramcontent.com/pod-product-compliance
Lightning Source LLC
Chambersburg PA
CBHW021957220426
43663CB00007B/845